Second Corinthians

DR. MAXWELL SHIMBA

Published in Manhattan, New York by Shimba Publishing, LLC.

Shimba Publishing LLC
Printed in the United States of America

First Printing Edition 2023

Table of Contents

Preface...vi

About Second Corinthians viii

CHAPTER 1

Comfort, Suffering, and the Faithfulness of God 1

CHAPTER 2

Forgiveness, Reconciliation, and the Triumph of Love.................. 18

CHAPTER 3

The Contrast Between the Old and New Covenants...................... 32

CHAPTER 4

The Nature of Christian Ministry 46

CHAPTER 5

The Hope of Eternal Life 59

CHAPTER 6

The Call to Holiness.. 74

CHAPTER 7

Reconciliation and Repentance 87

CHAPTER 8

The Grace of Giving 101

CHAPTER 9

Generosity in Giving and the Blessing that results from a Cheerful
and Purposeful act of Giving 118

CHAPTER 10

Authority and Spiritual Warfare 130

CHAPTER 11

Apostle Paul's Authority 143

CHAPTER 12

Boasting in Weakness, and the sufficiency of God's Grace 164

CHAPTER 13

Testing and Self-Examination 180
CONCLUSION 192

Preface

Preface to the Second Epistle to the Corinthians

In the annals of Christian literature, the Second Epistle to the Corinthians stands as a testament to the enduring faith, perseverance, and resilience of the early Christian community. Penned by the apostle Paul, this epistle is a remarkable window into the heart of a tireless apostle who faced numerous trials and tribulations while fervently spreading the message of Christ. It's a poignant account of his struggles, triumphs, and the deep theological truths that underpin the Christian faith.

As the Pauline corpus unfolds, this letter occupies a unique space. It is a continuation of Paul's correspondence with the church in Corinth, a community he had previously admonished, guided, and nurtured. Now, with the Second Epistle to the Corinthians, he writes with the intention of further reconciliation, teaching, and edification.

Within these pages, readers will encounter a rich tapestry of themes, including the nature of Christian ministry, the challenges faced by those who labor in the gospel, the principles of giving and stewardship, the call to holiness, and the power of God's grace in the face of adversity. At its heart, this epistle conveys profound lessons about the essence of faith, love, and Christian conduct.

As we delve into the Second Epistle to the Corinthians, let us remember the enduring relevance of its message. For in the struggles, the conflicts, and the triumphs of the apostle Paul, we find an enduring testament to the transformative power of faith and the boundless love of   God. May this epistle continue to inspire and guide believers, serving as a reminder that even in the face of hardship and uncertainty, God's grace is sufficient, and His strength is made perfect in weakness.

In the following pages, we invite you to explore the timeless wisdom, encouragement, and spiritual insights that the Second Epistle to the Corinthians offers. It is a letter that resonates through the centuries, reminding us of the enduring power of the Christian faith and the unwavering love of our Creator.

Please note that this preface is a creative composition and not a part of the original biblical text. It aims to introduce the themes and context of 2 Corinthians.

About Second Corinthians

The Book of 2 Corinthians was likely written by the apostle Paul during his missionary journeys, and most scholars believe it was composed around the mid-50s to early 60s AD. As for the location of its writing, it is generally believed to have been written in Macedonia or possibly Ephesus. This book is one of the New Testament letters (epistles) written by Paul to the church in Corinth, addressing various issues and providing spiritual guidance and encouragement to the Corinthians. The exact date and place of its writing may not be definitively determined, but it is commonly associated with Paul's missionary activities during that period.

In the Second Corinthians, the Apostle Paul was addressing the Christian community in Corinth. He wrote this letter to the Corinthians for several important reasons:

1. Pastoral Concern: Paul had a deep and abiding concern for the spiritual well-being of the Corinthian church. He had previously written 1 Corinthians to address various issues and challenges facing the Corinthians, and he continued to have a pastor's heart for their growth and maturity in the faith.

2. Reconciliation: The Corinthians had faced internal conflicts and issues, and Paul desired reconciliation and unity within the church. He urged them to resolve their differences, seek forgiveness, and restore relationships, fostering harmony and love within the Christian community.

3. Response to Critics: Paul also wrote Second Corinthians as a response to critics and detractors who questioned his apostolic authority and sincerity. He defended his ministry and explained his motives,

emphasizing his dedication to preaching the gospel and serving the Corinthians.

4. Collection for the Saints: Paul addressed the collection for the saints in Jerusalem, encouraging the Corinthians to contribute to the relief of needy Christians in Jerusalem. He saw this as an opportunity for the Corinthians to express their love and unity with believers in other regions.

5. Spiritual Growth: Throughout the letter, Paul sought to encourage the Corinthians in their spiritual growth. He emphasized the transformative power of the gospel and the role of the Holy Spirit in the lives of believers. He challenged them to live according to the teachings of Christ and to examine their faith.

6. Trinitarian Theology: Paul also delved into theological matters, including the nature of God, the person of Christ, and the work of the Holy Spirit. He highlighted the Trinitarian nature of God and the blessings that believers receive through their relationship with the Triune God.

Second Corinthians serves as a testament to Paul's pastoral care for the Corinthians and his dedication to the health and growth of the church. It addresses a wide range of issues and challenges facing the Corinthians while emphasizing the central themes of faith, love, reconciliation, and the transformative power of the gospel.

Theological Theme of Second Corinthians: The Sufficiency of God's Grace

Throughout the Second Epistle to the Corinthians, a powerful theological theme emerges: the sufficiency of God's grace. This theme underscores the idea that God's grace is not only abundant but also fully adequate to meet the needs of believers, no matter the challenges or difficulties they face. Several verses in 2 Corinthians support this theme:

1. Sufficiency in Affliction: "But he said to me, 'My grace is sufficient for you, for my power is made perfect in weakness.'" (2 Corinthians 12:9a, ESV)

This verse, in the context of Paul's "thorn in the flesh," illustrates how God's grace is sufficient even in times of personal affliction. It reveals that God's strength is most evident when we acknowledge our weakness and rely on His grace.

2. Sufficiency in Ministry: "Not that we are sufficient in ourselves to claim anything as coming from us, but our sufficiency is from God, who has made us sufficient to be ministers of a new covenant, not of the letter but of the Spirit. For the letter kills, but the Spirit gives life." (2 Corinthians 3:5-6, ESV)

These verses emphasize that the sufficiency for effective ministry doesn't come from human abilities but from God. God equips and empowers believers through His grace for the ministry of the new covenant, which is a ministry of life and the Spirit.

3. Sufficiency in Trials: "For as we share abundantly in Christ's sufferings, so through Christ we share abundantly in comfort too." (2 Corinthians 1:5, ESV)

Here, Paul discusses how God's grace provides comfort and sufficiency to believers in the midst of trials and sufferings. Believers are not left to face difficulties alone but are comforted through their connection with Christ.

4. Sufficiency in Giving: "You will be enriched in every way to be generous in every way, which through us will produce thanksgiving to God." (2 Corinthians 9:11, ESV)

These verses highlight the sufficiency of God's grace in the context of giving and stewardship. God's grace not only provides for the needs of believers but enables them to be generous and bless others.

5. Sufficiency in Weakness: "For when I am weak, then I am strong." (2 Corinthians 12:10b, ESV)

This verse reinforces the idea that in times of weakness, believers find their strength and sufficiency in God's grace. It's a reminder that God's grace is transformative, making believers strong even in their moments of human weakness.

The theological theme of the sufficiency of God's grace in 2 Corinthians highlights the richness and completeness of God's provision in all aspects of the Christian life—whether in personal trials, ministry, giving, or in acknowledging human weaknesses. This theme underscores the profound truth that believers can fully rely on the abundant and all-sufficient grace of God.

Chapter 1
Comfort, Suffering, and the Faithfulness of God

The theme of 2 Corinthians Chapter 1 is comfort, suffering, and the faithfulness of God. In this chapter, the apostle Paul addresses the Corinthians and speaks about the comfort he has received from God in the midst of his trials and sufferings.

Key themes in 2 Corinthians Chapter 1 include:

1. Comfort in Suffering: The central theme is the comfort that Paul and his companions have received from God in their trials and suffering. Paul shares how God comforts them so that they can, in turn, comfort others who are facing difficulties.

2. Suffering and Affliction: Paul mentions the sufferings and afflictions that he and his fellow workers have endured for the sake of the gospel. This emphasizes the challenges faced in their ministry.

3. God of All Comfort: The chapter highlights God as the source of all comfort. Paul emphasizes that God is the one who comforts the downcast and afflicted.

4. Sincerity and Transparency: Paul underscores the sincerity and transparency of his ministry. He assures the Corinthians that he has been honest and faithful in his dealings with them.

5. Prayer and Thanksgiving: Paul mentions his prayers for the Corinthians and his gratitude for their support and prayers on his behalf.

6. Promises of God: The chapter speaks of the promises of God and how they are fulfilled in Christ. Paul emphasizes the reliability of God's promises.

In summary, 2 Corinthians Chapter 1 focuses on the themes of comfort in suffering, the faithfulness of God, and the sincerity of Paul's ministry. It underscores the idea that God is the ultimate source of comfort and that the challenges and sufferings faced in ministry can be used to bring comfort and encouragement to others.

Verse 1 (2 Corinthians 1:1, KJV):

"Paul, an apostle of Jesus Christ by the will of God, and Timothy our brother, unto the church of God which is at Corinth, with all the saints which are in all Achaia:"

Expository Commentary on Verse 1:

Paul, an apostle of Jesus Christ by the will of God: The letter begins with Paul identifying himself as an apostle of Jesus Christ, emphasizing that his apostleship is not self-appointed but a result of God's divine will. This underscores the legitimacy and authority of his ministry. Paul was called by Christ on the road to Damascus (Acts 9:1-19), and his apostleship was confirmed through various means (2 Corinthians 12:12).

and Timothy our brother: Paul includes Timothy in the greeting, acknowledging him as a beloved fellow laborer in the gospel. Timothy was a young disciple of Paul who often accompanied him in his missionary journeys. His presence here signifies the unity and partnership in their ministry.

unto the church of God which is at Corinth: The letter is addressed to the Christian community in Corinth. "The church of God" highlights their belonging to God, indicating the divine origin and ownership of the church. This was a diverse congregation, facing various challenges and issues, which Paul would address throughout the letter.

with all the saints which are in all Achaia: Paul extends his greetings and blessing to all the believers in the broader region of Achaia, which encompassed not only Corinth but also other Christian communities in the area. This shows Paul's concern for the well-being and unity of the entire Christian body in the region.

Verse 2 (2 Corinthians 1:2, KJV):

"Grace be to you and peace from God our Father, and from the Lord Jesus Christ."

Expository Commentary on Verse 2:

Grace be to you: Paul opens with a familiar apostolic greeting, invoking God's grace upon the recipients. Grace, in the Christian context, represents God's unmerited favor and blessings. This is a reminder of the foundational Christian message of salvation by grace through faith (Ephesians 2:8-9).

and peace from God our Father: In addition to grace, Paul invokes peace upon the Corinthians. This peace is not merely the absence of conflict but a deep spiritual peace that comes from reconciliation with God. It signifies a harmonious relationship with God, obtained through Christ's atoning work on the cross (Romans 5:1).

and from the Lord Jesus Christ: The dual source of grace and peace is significant. It emphasizes the Trinitarian nature of the Christian faith. Grace and peace originate from both God the Father and the Lord Jesus Christ. This underscores the divinity of Christ and the role He plays in the believers' reconciliation with God.

In these opening verses, Paul establishes his authority as an apostle by emphasizing God's will, expresses his partnership with Timothy, addresses the recipients as the church of God, and invokes God's grace and peace upon them. These themes and concepts set the stage for the rest of the letter, where Paul will address various issues and challenges faced by the Corinthians.

Verse 3 (2 Corinthians 1:3, KJV):

"Blessed be God, even the Father of our Lord Jesus Christ, the Father of mercies, and the God of all comfort;"

Expository Commentary on Verse 3:

"Blessed be God, even the Father of our Lord Jesus Christ," - In this verse, Paul begins by offering praise to God, specifically referring to God as the Father of our Lord Jesus Christ. This title emphasizes the divine relationship within the Trinity, highlighting Jesus Christ's eternal divinity and God's role as the Father in the Godhead.

"the Father of mercies," - God is described as the source and origin of all mercies. This indicates that God is the One who bestows compassion, kindness, and compassion upon His people. It is a recognition of God's abundant and unfailing mercy toward humanity.

"and the God of all comfort;" - Paul also acknowledges God as the ultimate source of comfort. This comfort extends beyond emotional or physical comfort to encompass spiritual comfort. God provides solace and support to His people, especially in times of trouble and distress.

Verse 4 (2 Corinthians 1:4, KJV):

"Who comforteth us in all our tribulation, that we may be able to comfort them which are in any trouble, by the comfort wherewith we ourselves are comforted of God."

Expository Commentary on Verse 4:

"Who comforteth us in all our tribulation," - Paul emphasizes that God is the One who provides comfort to believers in the midst of their tribulations, trials, and hardships. This divine comfort is a reassurance that God is with His people during their difficult times, offering strength and solace.

"that we may be able to comfort them which are in any trouble," - Paul's experience of God's comfort is not just for his benefit. It equips him and other believers to be sources of comfort and encouragement to fellow Christians who are also facing difficulties. This reflects the principle of mutual support within the body of Christ.

"by the comfort wherewith we ourselves are comforted of God." - The comfort believers receive from God becomes a model for how they should comfort others. This highlights the idea that our personal experiences of God's comfort can be transformed into acts of compassion and support for others who are suffering.

Verse 5 (2 Corinthians 1:5, KJV):

"For as the sufferings of Christ abound in us, so our consolation also aboundeth by Christ."

Expository Commentary on Verse 5:

"For as the sufferings of Christ abound in us," - Paul acknowledges that as he and his fellow believers experience suffering and hardship in their lives, they share in the sufferings of Christ. This suggests that their sufferings are not in vain but are united with the sufferings of Christ for a greater purpose.

"so our consolation also aboundeth by Christ." - In parallel to the suffering, Paul points out that the consolation or comfort they receive is also abundant through Christ. This underscores the idea that the depth of suffering can be matched by the richness of divine consolation.

Verse 6 (2 Corinthians 1:6, KJV):

"And whether we be afflicted, it is for your consolation and salvation, which is effectual in the enduring of the same sufferings which we also suffer: or whether we be comforted, it is for your consolation and salvation."

Expository Commentary on Verse 6:

"And whether we be afflicted, it is for your consolation and salvation," - Paul explains that when he and his companions endure suffering, it is ultimately for the benefit of the Corinthians. Their suffering serves as an example and source of consolation and salvation for the Corinthians.

"which is effectual in the enduring of the same sufferings which we also suffer:" - Paul implies that the Corinthians can find inspiration and effectiveness in their faith by observing how he and his companions endure the same sufferings that the Corinthians are experiencing. This shows that their suffering can have a redemptive quality when it is endured in faith.

"or whether we be comforted, it is for your consolation and salvation." - Likewise, when Paul and his companions receive comfort and consolation from God, it is not for their sake alone but also for the spiritual well-being and salvation of the Corinthians. Their experiences, whether of suffering or comfort, are interconnected and meant to edify the broader Christian community.

Verse 7 (2 Corinthians 1:7, KJV):

"And our hope of you is stedfast, knowing, that as ye are partakers of the sufferings, so shall ye be also of the consolation."

Expository Commentary on Verse 7:

"And our hope of you is stedfast," - Paul expresses a firm and unwavering hope concerning the Corinthians. Despite the challenges and suffering they face, he has confidence in their faith and spiritual growth.

"knowing, that as ye are partakers of the sufferings, so shall ye be also of the consolation." - Paul assures the Corinthians that just as they share in the sufferings that are common to believers, they will also partake in the consolation and comfort provided by God. This reflects the principle that God's comfort is not limited to a select few but is available to all who endure hardships in faith.

In these verses, Paul emphasizes the character of God as the Father of mercies and the God of all comfort. He highlights the connection between suffering and comfort, underscoring the idea that believers can find strength and purpose in their trials, and that God's comfort is abundant and meant to be shared within the Christian community. This sets the stage for further discussions about suffering and the role of God's comfort in the following chapters of 2 Corinthians.

Verse 8 (2 Corinthians 1:8, KJV):

"For we would not, brethren, have you ignorant of our trouble which came to us in Asia, that we were pressed out of measure, above strength, insomuch that we despaired even of life."

Expository Commentary on Verse 8:

"For we would not, brethren, have you ignorant of our trouble which came to us in Asia," - Paul starts by expressing his desire for the Corinthians not to be unaware of the severe trouble and affliction he and his companions faced while in Asia. He's about to describe a challenging situation they endured.

"that we were pressed out of measure, above strength," - Paul vividly describes the intensity of the suffering they experienced. They were burdened beyond their own ability to endure, indicating that the trials were overwhelming and beyond human capacity to bear.

"insomuch that we despaired even of life." - The extremity of their circumstances led them to the point of despair, even to the extent of losing hope in life itself. This highlights the severity of the trials they encountered.

Verse 9 (2 Corinthians 1:9, KJV):
"But we had the sentence of death in ourselves, that we should not trust in ourselves, but in God which raiseth the dead:"

Expository Commentary on Verse 9:

"But we had the sentence of death in ourselves," - Paul acknowledges that they felt as though they had been condemned to death. Their situation was so dire that they believed they might not survive. This profound sense of impending death served a purpose in their spiritual journey.

"that we should not trust in ourselves," - The experience of facing death forced Paul and his companions to recognize the limitations of their own abilities and strength. They learned not to rely on their own resources but to look beyond themselves for help.

"but in God which raiseth the dead:" - This crisis pointed them to God as the ultimate source of hope and deliverance. They put their trust in the God who has the power to raise the dead, emphasizing God's sovereignty and ability to bring life even in the face of death.

Verse 10 (2 Corinthians 1:10, KJV):
"Who delivered us from so great a death, and doth deliver: in whom we trust that he will yet deliver us;"

Expository Commentary on Verse 10:

"Who delivered us from so great a death," - Paul acknowledges that God intervened and delivered them from the imminent threat of death that they faced. This highlights God's saving power in their lives.

"and doth deliver:" - Paul affirms that God continues to be their Deliverer, indicating that their reliance on Him is not limited to past events but extends to their present and future.

"in whom we trust that he will yet deliver us;" - This verse conveys a strong message of trust in God's faithfulness. Paul and his companions have confidence that God will continue to deliver them in the future, regardless of the challenges they may encounter. This trust is grounded in their understanding of God's character and past actions on their behalf.

Verse 11 (2 Corinthians 1:11, KJV):

"Ye also helping together by prayer for us, that for the gift bestowed upon us by the means of many persons thanks may be given by many on our behalf."

Expository Commentary on Verse 11:

"Ye also helping together by prayer for us," - Paul acknowledges the vital role of the Corinthians in supporting him and his companions. Their prayers are seen as a form of collaboration, where the Corinthians are actively participating in the work of God by interceding on behalf of the apostles.

"that for the gift bestowed upon us by the means of many persons," - The prayers of the Corinthians are viewed as a gift given by many individuals. This gift of prayer is an essential means through which God's grace and help are bestowed upon Paul and his team.

"thanks may be given by many on our behalf." - The ultimate goal of the Corinthians' prayers is to produce a response of thanksgiving from many people. The prayers offered by the Corinthians, along with God's deliverance, will result in praise and gratitude on behalf of Paul and his companions.

In these verses, Paul shares a deeply personal experience of suffering and despair, highlighting the importance of relying on God in times of extreme difficulty. He also emphasizes the role of the Corinthian believers in offering prayers and support, leading to thanksgiving and a stronger sense of community within the body of Christ. These verses serve as a powerful testimony to God's faithfulness and the significance of intercessory prayer within the Christian community.

Verse 12 (2 Corinthians 1:12, KJV):

"For our rejoicing is this, the testimony of our conscience, that in simplicity and godly sincerity, not with fleshly wisdom, but by the grace of God, we have had our conversation in the world, and more abundantly to you-ward."

Expository Commentary on Verse 12:

"For our rejoicing is this, the testimony of our conscience," - Paul begins this passage by expressing his joy and confidence in the testimony of his own conscience. He takes pride in the fact that his conscience bears witness to the integrity and sincerity of his actions and ministry.

"that in simplicity and godly sincerity," - Paul emphasizes the principles that guided his conduct and ministry. He acted with simplicity, meaning his actions were straightforward, without duplicity or hidden agendas. His sincerity was grounded in a deep reverence for God and a genuine commitment to righteousness and truth.

"not with fleshly wisdom, but by the grace of God," - Paul contrasts his approach with the world's wisdom, which often relies on human strategies and cunning. Instead, he emphasizes that his actions were guided by God's grace. His ministry was not about clever tactics but about relying on God's enabling power.

"we have had our conversation in the world," - The term "conversation" in the King James Version refers to one's way of life or behavior. Paul is saying that their way of life, including their actions and conduct, was a testimony to the world.

"and more abundantly to you-ward." - Paul also highlights the Corinthians, indicating that their relationship was marked by even greater sincerity and dedication, as he served them with special care and diligence.

Verse 13 (2 Corinthians 1:13, KJV):

"For we write none other things unto you than what ye read or acknowledge; and I trust ye shall acknowledge even to the end;"

Expository Commentary on Verse 13:

"For we write none other things unto you than what ye read or acknowledge;" - Paul emphasizes that there are no hidden or undisclosed messages in his letters to the Corinthians. Everything he writes to them is clear and straightforward. He is not attempting to deceive or manipulate them.

"and I trust ye shall acknowledge even to the end;" - Paul expresses his confidence that the Corinthians will continue to recognize the truth of his words and intentions. He expects their understanding and acknowledgment to endure, indicating his trust in their spiritual growth and discernment.

Verse 14 (2 Corinthians 1:14, KJV):

"As also ye have acknowledged us in part, that we are your rejoicing, even as ye also are ours in the day of the Lord Jesus."

Expository Commentary on Verse 14:

"As also ye have acknowledged us in part," - Paul acknowledges that the Corinthians have partially recognized him and his companions for who they are and the role they play in their lives. This suggests that there may have been some misunderstandings or incomplete recognition.

"that we are your rejoicing," - Paul emphasizes that he and his companions are a source of rejoicing for the Corinthians. They should take pride in their relationship and the ministry that Paul has undertaken among them.

"even as ye also are ours in the day of the Lord Jesus." - Paul reciprocates the sentiment by stating that the Corinthians are also a source of rejoicing for him. He looks forward to the day of the Lord Jesus, likely referring to the future return of Christ, when both he and the Corinthians will rejoice together in the fullness of their relationship.

In these verses, Paul reflects on the sincerity and integrity of his ministry, emphasizing that it is guided by godly principles and the grace of God. He reassures the Corinthians of the transparency of his communication and his confidence in their understanding. The passage also underscores the mutual rejoicing and the significant relationship between Paul and the Corinthians, which will find its ultimate fulfillment in the day of the Lord Jesus.

Verse 15 (2 Corinthians 1:15, KJV):

"And in this confidence I was minded to come unto you before, that ye might have a second benefit;"

Expository Commentary on Verse 15:

"And in this confidence I was minded to come unto you before," - Paul begins this section by referring to his initial intention to visit the Corinthians. He had been confident and determined to come to them earlier.

"that ye might have a second benefit;" - Paul's desire for an earlier visit was driven by the hope that the Corinthians would receive a second benefit from his presence. This implies that he had previously visited them and desired to return for their further spiritual growth and edification.

Verse 16 (2 Corinthians 1:16, KJV):

"And to pass by you into Macedonia, and to come again out of Macedonia unto you, and of you to be brought on my way toward Judaea."

Expository Commentary on Verse 16:

"And to pass by you into Macedonia," - Paul's initial travel plans included passing through Corinth on his way to Macedonia. This suggests that Corinth was on the route of his intended journey.

"and to come again out of Macedonia unto you," - After visiting Macedonia, Paul planned to return to Corinth, indicating his strong connection and commitment to this church and community.

"and of you to be brought on my way toward Judaea." - Paul also anticipated that the Corinthians would assist him in his journey to Judea. They would play a part in supporting him as he continued his missionary work in that region.

Verse 17 (2 Corinthians 1:17, KJV):

"When I, therefore, was thus minded, did I use lightness? or the things that I purpose, do I purpose according to the flesh, that with me there should be yea yea, and nay nay?"

Expository Commentary on Verse 17:

"When I, therefore, was thus minded," - Paul reflects on his earlier intentions and plans, emphasizing his state of mind at that time.

"did I use lightness?" - Paul raises a rhetorical question, asking if he was acting with fickleness or frivolity in his intentions to visit Corinth. In other words, he is challenging any accusation of inconsistency.

"or the things that I purpose, do I purpose according to the flesh," - He further inquires whether his plans are grounded in human, worldly motives or if they are merely based on self-interest and worldly considerations.

"that with me there should be yea yea, and nay nay?" - Paul's intent in these questions is to establish his commitment to truth and consistency. He insists that his words and actions are not characterized by vacillation or duplicity but are rooted in sincerity and truth.

In these verses, Paul discusses his earlier plans to visit the Corinthians and the integrity of his intentions. He addresses the criticism of being inconsistent or using "lightness" in his decision-making and asserts that his purposes are sincere and grounded in spiritual motivation, not driven by worldly concerns. This section reflects Paul's desire for transparent and steadfast ministry and his effort to clarify his actions and motives to the Corinthians.

Verse 18 (2 Corinthians 1:18, KJV):

"But as God is true, our word toward you was not yea and nay."

Expository Commentary on Verse 18:

"But as God is true," - Paul begins this section by appealing to the truth and faithfulness of God. He uses this phrase to emphasize the reliability and consistency of God's character.

"our word toward you was not yea and nay." - Paul assures the Corinthians that their communication with them was not characterized by mixed messages or vacillation. In other words, he is declaring that their message was consistent and truthful.

This verse serves as a reassurance to the Corinthians that their apostolic message and communication with them have been marked by integrity and sincerity.

Verse 19 (2 Corinthians 1:19, KJV):

"For the Son of God, Jesus Christ, who was preached among you by us, even by me and Silvanus and Timotheus, was not yea and nay, but in him was yea."

Expository Commentary on Verse 19:

"For the Son of God, Jesus Christ, who was preached among you by us," - Paul highlights the central message they preached to the Corinthians, which was the Son of God, Jesus Christ. This underscores the importance of the gospel message in their ministry.

"even by me and Silvanus and Timotheus," - Paul identifies himself and his companions, Silvanus (Silas) and Timothy, as the ones who delivered this message. Their unified proclamation of the gospel adds to its credibility.

"was not yea and nay, but in him was yea." - Paul contrasts their message with ambiguity and consistency. The message of Jesus Christ was not characterized by mixed signals; it was unwaveringly true. In Christ, all God's promises find their "yes" or fulfillment.

This verse emphasizes the consistency and truthfulness of the message of Jesus Christ as preached by Paul and his companions.

Verse 20 (2 Corinthians 1:20, KJV):

"For all the promises of God in him are yea, and in him Amen, unto the glory of God by us."

Expository Commentary on Verse 20:

"For all the promises of God in him are yea," - This verse affirms that all the promises of God find their affirmation or "yes" in Christ. In other words, every promise God has made is fulfilled and affirmed through Jesus Christ.

"and in him Amen," - Not only are God's promises "yes" in Christ, but they are also "Amen" in Him. The term "Amen" signifies certainty, affirmation, and truth. This further underscores the reliability of God's promises in Christ.

"unto the glory of God by us." - The purpose of these affirmed and certain promises is to bring glory to God through the ministry of apostles like Paul. It is through their faithful proclamation of the gospel and the fulfillment of God's promises in Christ that God's glory is revealed.

This verse emphasizes the foundational role of Jesus Christ in fulfilling and affirming God's promises and highlights the purpose of this affirmation: to bring glory to God through the work of apostles and believers.

Verse 21 (2 Corinthians 1:21, KJV):

"Now he which stablisheth us with you in Christ, and hath anointed us, is God;"

Expository Commentary on Verse 21:

"Now he which stablisheth us with you in Christ," - Paul points to the One who establishes and strengthens both himself and the Corinthians in their shared faith in Christ. The term "us with you" emphasizes the unity and common faith shared by Paul and the Corinthian believers.

"and hath anointed us, is God;" - This anointing is a reference to the empowering and setting apart of believers for their service in Christ. It is not by human wisdom or effort but by the work of God Himself.

This verse underscores that it is God who strengthens and equips believers for their service in Christ, emphasizing the divine origin and empowerment of their ministry.

Verse 22 (2 Corinthians 1:22, KJV):

"Who hath also sealed us, and given the earnest of the Spirit in our hearts."

Expository Commentary on Verse 22:

"Who hath also sealed us," - God not only establishes and anoints believers but also seals them. This sealing is a mark of ownership and security, signifying that believers belong to God and are protected by Him.

"and given the earnest of the Spirit in our hearts." - As a further confirmation and assurance, God has given the Holy Spirit to dwell in the hearts of believers. The Holy Spirit serves as a guarantee or "earnest" of the future inheritance and blessings promised to believers.

This verse highlights the comprehensive work of God in equipping and securing believers through the sealing and indwelling of the Holy Spirit, ensuring their identity as God's children and their future inheritance.

In these verses, Paul underscores the reliability and consistency of the message they preached, which was centered on Jesus Christ. He emphasizes that all of God's promises are affirmed in Christ and that it is God who establishes, anoints, seals, and provides the Holy Spirit to believers, guaranteeing their future inheritance. This passage reaffirms the trustworthiness of God's work in the lives of believers and the centrality of Christ in the fulfillment of God's promises.

Verse 23 (2 Corinthians 1:23, KJV):

"Moreover, I call God for a record upon my soul, that to spare you I came not as yet unto Corinth."

Expository Commentary on Verse 23:

"Moreover, I call God for a record upon my soul," - In this verse, Paul appeals to God as a witness to the sincerity of his intentions and actions. He solemnly swears that his actions are in line with his stated purpose.

"that to spare you I came not as yet unto Corinth." - Paul clarifies that his decision to delay his visit to Corinth was made with the intention of sparing them. It is likely that he wanted to avoid a potentially difficult confrontation or disciplinary action during his initial visit.

Paul emphasizes that his actions and decisions are not arbitrary but are made with careful consideration and accountability to God. His desire is to act in the best interest of the Corinthians, even if it means postponing his visit.

Verse 24 (2 Corinthians 1:24, KJV):

"Not for that we have dominion over your faith, but are helpers of your joy: for by faith ye stand."

Expository Commentary on Verse 24:

"Not for that we have dominion over your faith," - Paul clarifies his role as an apostle. He wants the Corinthians to understand that his authority is not about exercising control or dominance over their faith. He does not seek to be a dictator or to lord over their beliefs.

"but are helpers of your joy:" - Instead, Paul's role is to assist and support the Corinthians in their faith journey. He sees his ministry as contributing to their joy and spiritual well-being. His aim is to be a source of encouragement and support.

"for by faith ye stand." - Paul's ultimate goal is to help the Corinthians stand strong in their faith. He acknowledges that their faith is the foundation upon which they are established. Their faith empowers them to withstand challenges and remain steadfast in their Christian walk.

In these verses, Paul clarifies his decision to delay his visit to Corinth, emphasizing that his actions are made with the Corinthians' best interests in mind and are accountable to God. He also highlights the nature of his apostolic authority as a support and helper of their faith, with the ultimate goal of aiding their joy and strengthening their standing in faith. This passage underscores the servant leadership style of the apostle Paul and his commitment to nurturing the faith and well-being of the Corinthian believers.

Chapter 2

Forgiveness, Reconciliation, and the Triumph of Love

The theme of 2 Corinthians Chapter 2 is forgiveness, reconciliation, and the triumph of love. In this chapter, the apostle Paul discusses the concept of forgiveness and reconciliation within the Christian community and the importance of expressing love and support for one another.

Key themes in 2 Corinthians Chapter 2 include:

1. Forgiveness and Reconciliation: The central theme is the concept of forgiveness and reconciliation. Paul addresses an issue of discipline within the Corinthian church and encourages the church to forgive and comfort the one who had faced discipline. He highlights the importance of restoring a repentant member to fellowship.

2. Triumph of Love: Paul speaks of the triumph of love in the context of the situation he is addressing. He encourages the church to reaffirm their love for the individual who had faced discipline, emphasizing that love should prevail in Christian relationships.

3. Spiritual Warfare and Deception: The chapter alludes to the idea of spiritual warfare and the potential for deception by Satan. Paul

mentions the need to be vigilant and discerning to avoid being outwitted by the schemes of the enemy.

4. Ministerial Triumph: Paul expresses his confidence that his ministry in Corinth has been a triumph in Christ. He views the positive response of the Corinthians to his message as a victory.

5. Fragrance of Christ: Paul uses the metaphor of believers being a fragrance of Christ to God. He describes the aroma of Christ that is perceived by those who are being saved and those who are perishing.

In summary, 2 Corinthians Chapter 2 centers around the themes of forgiveness, reconciliation, the triumph of love, and the importance of expressing love and support within the Christian community. It underscores the need for forgiveness and restoration within the body of believers and the victory of love over division and discord.

Verse 1 (2 Corinthians 2:1, KJV):

"But I determined this with myself, that I would not come again to you in heaviness."

Expository Commentary on Verse 1:

"But I determined this with myself," - Paul begins by stating that he had made a personal decision. He had given careful thought and consideration to his actions and choices regarding his relationship with the Corinthians.

"that I would not come again to you in heaviness." - Paul's decision was rooted in his desire not to cause the Corinthians additional sorrow or distress during his visit. This may imply that his previous visit to Corinth had been challenging or sorrowful for both him and the Corinthians.

Paul's intention is to foster a more positive and constructive interaction with the Corinthians, one that would not be characterized by heaviness or sorrow.

Verse 2 (2 Corinthians 2:2, KJV):

"For if I make you sorry, who is he then that maketh me glad, but the same which is made sorry by me?"

Expository Commentary on Verse 2:

"For if I make you sorry," - Paul acknowledges the possibility that his previous visit or actions may have caused sorrow among the Corinthians. He's sensitive to the impact of his ministry on their emotions.

"who is he then that maketh me glad," - Paul rhetorically questions who would bring him joy or happiness if his ministry leads to sorrow among the Corinthians. He recognizes the deep connection between his well-being and the spiritual well-being of the Corinthians.

"but the same which is made sorry by me?" - Paul's joy is closely tied to the spiritual condition and happiness of the Corinthians. If he brings sorrow, the only way for him to experience joy is by seeing their spiritual health and happiness restored.

This verse illustrates the close bond between Paul and the Corinthian believers. He is deeply invested in their well-being and is conscious of the impact his ministry has on their emotional and spiritual state.

Verse 3 (2 Corinthians 2:3, KJV):

"And I wrote this same unto you, lest, when I came, I should have sorrow from them of whom I ought to rejoice; having confidence in you all, that my joy is the joy of you all."

Expository Commentary on Verse 3:

"And I wrote this same unto you," - Paul refers to a previous letter (possibly 1 Corinthians) that conveyed the same sentiments. He had written to them to express his concerns and intentions.

"lest, when I came, I should have sorrow from them of whom I ought to rejoice;" - Paul's writing was motivated by the desire to prevent a situation where, upon his arrival in Corinth, he would encounter sorrow from those he should have been able to rejoice with. He wanted to avoid any conflict or discord that would hinder the joy he should have in their presence.

"having confidence in you all, that my joy is the joy of you all." - Paul's confidence in the Corinthians is evident. He believes that his joy and their joy are interconnected. He anticipates a joyful and harmonious relationship with the Corinthians based on their mutual faith and commitment.

This verse reflects Paul's pastoral concern for maintaining positive and joyful relationships with the Corinthians and the importance of clear communication to avoid misunderstandings or conflicts.

Verse 4 (2 Corinthians 2:4, KJV):

"For out of much affliction and anguish of heart I wrote unto you with many tears; not that ye should be grieved, but that ye might know the love which I have more abundantly unto you."

Expository Commentary on Verse 4:

"For out of much affliction and anguish of heart I wrote unto you with many tears;" - Paul reveals the emotional and heartfelt nature of the letter he had written to the Corinthians. He describes the deep sorrow and anguish he experienced while composing it, suggesting that the issues he addressed were profoundly distressing to him.

"not that ye should be grieved," - It's essential to note that Paul's intention in writing the letter was not to cause grief or pain to the Corinthians. The sorrow he experienced was not his goal but a byproduct of his deep concern for their spiritual well-being.

"but that ye might know the love which I have more abundantly unto you." - Instead, the primary purpose of the letter was to convey the depth of his love for them. He wanted them to understand the extent of his care and affection, which he felt had grown even more abundant over time.

This verse provides insight into the emotional and personal nature of Paul's ministry and his motivation for addressing difficult issues with the Corinthians. His deep love for them prompted him to address their concerns, even though it was a painful and tearful process.

Verse 5 (2 Corinthians 2:5, KJV):

"But if any have caused grief, he hath not grieved me, but in part: that I may not overcharge you all."

Expository Commentary on Verse 5:

"But if any have caused grief," - Paul acknowledges that there has been an individual or individuals who have caused sorrow or distress within the Corinthian church. He is addressing a specific issue or person that has been a source of trouble.

"he hath not grieved me, but in part:" - Paul clarifies that this person's actions have not primarily caused him personal grief, but rather have brought sorrow to the community of believers. He seeks to distinguish between his own feelings and the collective impact of this individual's actions.

"that I may not overcharge you all." - Paul's motivation in addressing this issue is to prevent an excessive or undue burden on the entire Corinthian congregation. He wants to ensure that the disciplinary action is appropriately targeted and does not unnecessarily burden the entire church.

Paul's approach here demonstrates his pastoral care for the Corinthian believers. He's concerned about the negative influence of this individual's actions on the whole community and seeks to address it effectively.

Verse 6 (2 Corinthians 2:6, KJV):

"Sufficient to such a man is this punishment, which was inflicted of many."

Expository Commentary on Verse 6:

"Sufficient to such a man is this punishment," - Paul believes that the disciplinary action taken against the individual in question has been adequate. The punishment that was imposed by the Corinthian church has served its purpose.

"which was inflicted of many." - The punishment was not the result of Paul's personal judgment or decision but was carried out by the consensus and participation of many individuals within the church. This underscores the communal aspect of church discipline.

Paul recognizes the effectiveness of the disciplinary action taken by the Corinthian congregation and is satisfied with the response to the situation.

Verse 7 (2 Corinthians 2:7, KJV):

"So that contrariwise ye ought rather to forgive him, and comfort him, lest perhaps such a one should be swallowed up with overmuch sorrow."

Expository Commentary on Verse 7:

"So that contrariwise ye ought rather to forgive him, and comfort him," - Paul's emphasis shifts to the necessity of forgiveness and comfort. He encourages the Corinthians to take the opposite approach now. Instead of continued discipline, they should extend forgiveness and offer consolation to the individual who had been disciplined.

"lest perhaps such a one should be swallowed up with overmuch sorrow." - The reason for this change in approach is the concern that the individual might be overwhelmed by excessive sorrow if they are not forgiven and comforted. Paul is advocating for a restorative approach, showing care for the individual's well-being and spiritual recovery.

Paul's pastoral wisdom is evident in his recommendation to the Corinthians. He recognizes the need for both discipline and restoration in the church, depending on the circumstances and the well-being of the individual involved.

Verse 8 (2 Corinthians 2:8, KJV):

"Wherefore I beseech you that ye would confirm your love toward him."

Expository Commentary on Verse 8:

"Wherefore I beseech you that ye would confirm your love toward him." - Paul earnestly implores the Corinthians to reaffirm their love and affection for the disciplined individual. He wants them to demonstrate their care and support for his spiritual restoration.

Paul's appeal here underscores the importance of love, grace, and reconciliation within the Christian community. He encourages the Corinthians to express their love and commitment to the individual, reflecting the heart of the Gospel.

Verse 9 (2 Corinthians 2:9, KJV):

"For to this end also did I write, that I might know the proof of you, whether ye be obedient in all things."

Expository Commentary on Verse 9:

"For to this end also did I write," - Paul clarifies that one of the purposes of his previous letter, in which he addressed the issue and disciplinary action, was to test the obedience and faithfulness of the Corinthians in responding to such matters.

"that I might know the proof of you," - By addressing this issue and observing how the Corinthians would respond, Paul sought to test or assess their faithfulness, sincerity, and willingness to obey apostolic counsel.

"whether ye be obedient in all things." - Paul's concern extends beyond the specific case at hand. He is interested in whether the

Corinthians will demonstrate obedience and faithfulness in all matters, not just in this particular instance.

Paul's writing and guidance aim to foster obedience and faithfulness within the Corinthian church, challenging them to demonstrate their commitment to the principles of the Gospel.

Certainly! Here is an expository study and comprehensive commentary on 2 Corinthians Chapter 2, verse 10, using the King James Bible with references:

Verse 10 (2 Corinthians 2:10, KJV):

"To whom ye forgive any thing, I forgive also: for if I forgave any thing, to whom I forgave it, for your sakes forgave I it in the person of Christ;"

Expository Commentary on Verse 10:

In this verse, Paul discusses the act of forgiveness and its significance within the Christian community.

- "To whom ye forgive any thing, I forgive also:" - Paul begins by acknowledging the Corinthians' role in forgiving someone. He recognizes their authority and ability to forgive within their congregation.

- "for if I forgave any thing, to whom I forgave it," - Paul emphasizes his own willingness to forgive. He implies that he has already extended forgiveness to someone.

- "for your sakes forgave I it in the person of Christ;" - Here, Paul provides the underlying reason for his forgiveness. He forgave not only for the sake of the individual involved but also for the sake of the Corinthian community. Moreover, he mentions forgiving "in the person of Christ," indicating that his forgiveness is in alignment with the example and teachings of Christ, who taught forgiveness and reconciliation.

Key Points:

1. Recognition of the Corinthians' Role: Paul acknowledges the Corinthians' role in the act of forgiveness. This recognition of their authority and responsibility within the church community is an important aspect of their Christian life.

2. Paul's Willingness to Forgive: Paul makes it clear that he has already forgiven someone. This suggests that he is actively engaged in addressing issues of conflict and wrongdoing within the church.

3. Forgiveness for the Sake of the Community: Paul's motivation for forgiveness goes beyond the individual involved. He forgives for the sake of the Corinthian community, emphasizing the importance of unity and reconciliation within the body of believers.

4. Forgiveness in the Name of Christ: Paul's reference to forgiving "in the person of Christ" underscores the central role of Christ's teachings and example in matters of forgiveness. It reflects the Christian ethic of forgiveness as a reflection of Christ's love and grace.

This verse highlights the significance of forgiveness in the Christian community, emphasizing the need for reconciliation and unity. It also demonstrates the pastoral care of Paul as he works to address issues of conflict and division within the Corinthian church.

Verse 11 (2 Corinthians 2:11, KJV):

"Lest Satan should get an advantage of us: for we are not ignorant of his devices."

Expository Commentary on Verse 11:

In this verse, Paul addresses the Corinthians' awareness of Satan's schemes and the need for vigilance in spiritual matters.

- "Lest Satan should get an advantage of us:" - Paul expresses concern that Satan, the adversary and deceiver, might gain an advantage over the Corinthians or the Christian community as a whole. He acknowledges the reality of spiritual warfare and the potential for harm.

- "for we are not ignorant of his devices." - Paul assures the Corinthians that they are not uninformed or ignorant concerning Satan's tactics and strategies. He implies that they have received knowledge and understanding about the schemes and deceptions of the evil one. This knowledge equips them to resist and defend against Satan's efforts to undermine their faith and unity.

Key Points:

1. Awareness of Spiritual Warfare: Paul underscores the existence of spiritual warfare in the Christian life. He acknowledges the very real presence of Satan, who seeks to disrupt and divide the Christian community.

2. Need for Vigilance: The apostle emphasizes the need for vigilance and awareness among believers. Ignorance of Satan's devices can lead to vulnerability, so it is crucial for Christians to be alert and discerning in their faith.

3. Knowledge of Satan's Schemes: Paul suggests that the Corinthians have received instruction and knowledge about Satan's devices. This knowledge enables them to recognize and resist the enemy's tactics, thereby safeguarding their faith and unity.

This verse serves as a reminder of the spiritual battle that Christians face and the importance of being informed and discerning in order to protect the church from the schemes of the evil one. It also highlights the role of spiritual knowledge and awareness in maintaining the unity and strength of the Christian community.

Verse 12 (2 Corinthians 2:12, KJV):

"Furthermore, when I came to Troas to preach Christ's gospel, and a door was opened unto me of the Lord,"

Expository Commentary on Verse 12:

"Furthermore, when I came to Troas to preach Christ's gospel," - Paul begins this section by recounting his visit to Troas. He had traveled to this city with the specific purpose of proclaiming the gospel of Christ. Troas was a significant port city in the Roman province of Asia, located on the Aegean Sea.

"and a door was opened unto me of the Lord," - Paul acknowledges that an opportunity for ministry was divinely provided by the Lord. The phrase "a door was opened" is a metaphorical expression indicating that a favorable opportunity for preaching the gospel had arisen. This implies that circumstances were conducive to his ministry.

This verse highlights the apostle Paul's commitment to spreading the message of Christ and his recognition of the divine guidance and opportunities in his missionary work.

Verse 13 (2 Corinthians 2:13, KJV):

"I had no rest in my spirit because I found not Titus my brother, but taking my leave of them, I went from thence into Macedonia."

Expository Commentary on Verse 13:

"I had no rest in my spirit because I found not Titus my brother," - Paul conveys his emotional state during his stay in Troas. He was restless and anxious, primarily because he had not encountered Titus, a close associate and fellow worker in the ministry. Paul had likely sent Titus to Corinth with a previous letter, and he was eagerly awaiting Titus's return with news from the Corinthian church.

"but taking my leave of them, I went from thence into Macedonia." - Due to his concern and restlessness over not finding Titus and receiving the expected report, Paul decided to leave Troas and continue his journey into Macedonia. This decision was driven by his desire to seek information about the situation in Corinth and the Corinthians' response to his previous letter.

This verse provides insight into Paul's emotional and relational aspects of his ministry. He was deeply concerned about the well-being of the Corinthian believers and sought to maintain close communication and connection with them, even to the point of altering his travel plans. It demonstrates his pastoral care and concern for the churches he founded and nurtured.

Verse 14 (2 Corinthians 2:14, KJV):

"Now thanks be unto God, which always causeth us to triumph in Christ and maketh manifest the savor of his knowledge by us in every place."

Expository Commentary on Verse 14:

"Now thanks be unto God," - Paul begins this passage with an expression of gratitude and thanksgiving to God. He acknowledges God as the source of all his triumph and success in his ministry.

"which always causeth us to triumph in Christ," - Paul emphasizes the consistent pattern of triumph and victory that he experiences in Christ. It is through his faith and reliance on Christ that he continually overcomes challenges and obstacles in his ministry.

"and maketh manifest the savor of his knowledge by us in every place." - Paul describes the impact of his ministry as making the fragrance or aroma of the knowledge of God evident to all people, wherever he goes. In other words, his preaching and service spread the knowledge of God's truth.

This verse reflects Paul's deep sense of gratitude for the success of his ministry, which is attributed to God, and underscores the idea that his work results in the spread of the knowledge of Christ's gospel.

Verse 15 (2 Corinthians 2:15, KJV):

"For we are unto God a sweet savor of Christ, in them that are saved, and in them that perish."

Expository Commentary on Verse 15:

"For we are unto God a sweet savor of Christ," - Paul uses the imagery of a fragrant offering to describe the nature of their ministry. To God, the service of Paul and his companions is like a pleasing aroma of Christ. This suggests that their work is acceptable and well-pleasing to God.

"in them that are saved, and in them that perish." - Paul's ministry, symbolized by the sweet savor of Christ, has a different impact on different groups of people. It is received with acceptance and life by those who are saved, but it is a message of judgment and condemnation to those who reject it and, as a result, "perish."

This verse underscores the dual impact of the gospel: it brings salvation to some and judgment to others, depending on their response.

Verse 16 (2 Corinthians 2:16, KJV):

"To the one we are the savor of death unto death, and to the other the savor of life unto life. And who is sufficient for these things?"

Expository Commentary on Verse 16:

"To the one we are the savor of death unto death," - Paul reiterates the dual effect of their ministry. To those who reject the gospel, their message is like a fragrance of death that leads to spiritual death, symbolizing the condemnation and judgment faced by those who persist in unbelief.

"and to the other the savor of life unto life." - On the contrary, to those who accept the message of Christ, their ministry is like a fragrant offering that leads to eternal life, symbolizing the spiritual rebirth and salvation that believers experience.

"And who is sufficient for these things?" - Paul acknowledges the weight and significance of their ministry. He raises a rhetorical question, highlighting the immense responsibility of being messengers of life and death. No one, in themselves, is sufficient for this task, but their sufficiency comes from God.

This verse emphasizes the profound impact of the gospel message on individuals, leading either to life or death, and underscores the need for divine empowerment in their ministry.

Verse 17 (2 Corinthians 2:17, KJV):

"For we are not as many, which corrupt the word of God: but as of sincerity, but as of God, in the sight of God speak we in Christ."

Expository Commentary on Verse 17:

"For we are not as many, which corrupt the word of God:" - Paul distinguishes his ministry from that of some others who engage in corrupting or distorting the word of God. These individuals are not faithful in their handling of the Scriptures and the gospel message.

"but as of sincerity," - Paul contrasts their approach with his own, emphasizing the sincerity of his ministry. He is genuine, honest, and straightforward in his presentation of the gospel.

"but as of God, in the sight of God speak we in Christ." - Paul anchors the integrity of his ministry in his relationship with God. He affirms that he speaks as a representative of God in Christ, with divine authorization and accountability. His ministry is characterized by truth and faithfulness, not manipulation or deceit.

This verse highlights the importance of sincerity and faithfulness in the proclamation of the gospel, contrasting the integrity of Paul's ministry with those who distort or manipulate God's Word for their own purposes.

Chapter 3
The Contrast Between the Old and New Covenants

The theme of 2 Corinthians Chapter 3 is the contrast between the old and new covenants, the ministry of the Spirit, and the glory of God revealed in Christ. In this chapter, the apostle Paul discusses the superiority of the new covenant and the transformative work of the Holy Spirit.

Key themes in 2 Corinthians Chapter 3 include:

1. New Covenant vs. Old Covenant: The central theme is the contrast between the old covenant, represented by the Mosaic law, and the new covenant established through Jesus Christ. Paul emphasizes the superiority of the new covenant, which is characterized by the Spirit rather than the letter of the law.

2. Ministers of the New Covenant: Paul describes himself and his fellow ministers as servants of the new covenant. They serve not with written laws but with the Spirit, emphasizing the transformative power of the gospel.

3. The Ministry of the Spirit: The chapter highlights the ministry of the Spirit as a key feature of the new covenant. It brings life and freedom, and it enables believers to reflect the glory of the Lord as they are transformed into His image.

4. The Veiled and Unveiled Glory: Paul speaks of the glory of God, which was veiled in the old covenant but is now unveiled in the new covenant through Christ. This glory leads to a greater boldness and openness in the ministry of the gospel.

5. Transformation and Renewal: The chapter emphasizes the transformative work of the Spirit, changing the hearts and minds of believers and renewing them into the image of Christ.

6. Freedom and Liberty: Paul speaks of the liberty and freedom that come through the Spirit, contrasting this with the bondage and veil of the old covenant.

In summary, 2 Corinthians Chapter 3 explores the themes of the old and new covenants, the ministry of the Spirit, the glory of God revealed in Christ, and the transformation and freedom found in the new covenant. It underscores the superiority of the new covenant in bringing life, liberty, and a deeper understanding of God's glory.

Verse 1 (2 Corinthians 3:1, KJV):

"Do we begin again to commend ourselves? Or need we, as some others, epistles of commendation to you, or letters of commendation from you?"

Expository Commentary on Verse 1:

"Do we begin again to commend ourselves?" - Paul starts this chapter by addressing the question of self-commendation. He's essentially asking whether he needs to reintroduce himself and his credentials to the Corinthians. This question may be prompted by the ongoing challenges and criticisms he has faced in his ministry.

"Or need we, as some others, epistles of commendation to you, or letters of commendation from you?" - Paul contrasts his approach with that of some other individuals in the early Christian community. These "others" were accustomed to providing or seeking written recommendations or commendations. Paul inquires whether he should engage in the same practice.

In this verse, Paul is addressing the issue of self-commendation and highlighting the contrast between his ministry and the practices of some others who relied on written endorsements or commendations. Paul's approach to ministry emphasizes the transformation of lives through the gospel, as we'll see in the following verses.

Verse 2 (2 Corinthians 3:2, KJV):

"Ye are our epistle written in our hearts, known and read of all men:"

Expository Commentary on Verse 2:

"Ye are our epistle written in our hearts," - Paul makes a profound statement about the Corinthian believers. He refers to them as the "epistle" or letter that is written on his heart. This means that the evidence of his ministry and the impact of the gospel are not found in written recommendations but in the transformed lives of the Corinthians. They are a living testament to the effectiveness of his ministry.

"known and read of all men:" - The transformed lives of the Corinthians are not hidden; they are evident and observable by all people. The impact of the gospel in their lives is like an open letter that can be "read" by anyone who encounters them.

In this verse, Paul shifts the focus from written commendations to the transformed lives of the Corinthian believers. He emphasizes the authenticity and impact of his ministry through the tangible transformation in the lives of those he has served.

Verse 3 (2 Corinthians 3:3, KJV):

"Forasmuch as ye are manifestly declared to be the epistle of Christ ministered by us, written not with ink, but with the Spirit of the living God; not in tables of stone, but in fleshy tables of the heart."

Expository Commentary on Verse 3:

"Forasmuch as ye are manifestly declared to be the epistle of Christ ministered by us," - Paul elaborates on the idea introduced in the previous verse. He affirms that the Corinthians are indeed the "epistle of Christ," a letter written by Christ Himself through Paul's ministry. This underscores the idea that the transformed lives of believers are a testament to Christ's work through the apostles.

"written not with ink, but with the Spirit of the living God;" - Paul emphasizes that this letter of transformation is not written with physical ink but with the power of the Holy Spirit, who is the living God. The work of the Spirit in the lives of believers is the true agent of this transformation.

"not in tables of stone, but in fleshy tables of the heart." - Paul contrasts the transformation of believers with the old covenant, symbolized by the Ten Commandments written on stone tablets. In the new covenant, the law of God is written not on external tablets but on the hearts of believers, signifying a profound inner transformation and a change of heart.

This verse underscores the divine nature of the transformation in the lives of believers. The Holy Spirit, not external rules or recommendations, is the agent of change, and this transformation is internal, written on the hearts of those who have received the gospel. It highlights the significance of the new covenant and the work of the Spirit in the lives of Christians.

Verse 4 (2 Corinthians 3:4, KJV):

"And such trust have we through Christ to God-ward:"

Expository Commentary on Verse 4:

"And such trust have we through Christ to God-ward:" - In this verse, Paul highlights the trust and confidence he and his fellow workers have. This trust is directed "through Christ to God-ward," indicating that their confidence is founded on their faith in Christ and their relationship with God.

Paul's ministry is rooted in trust and confidence in the Lord Jesus Christ, and he relies on this trust as the foundation of his work.

Verse 5 (2 Corinthians 3:5, KJV):

"Not that we are sufficient of ourselves to think anything as of ourselves; but our sufficiency is of God;"

Expository Commentary on Verse 5:

"Not that we are sufficient of ourselves to think anything as of ourselves;" - Paul makes it clear that he does not claim self-sufficiency or self-adequacy. He does not attribute any of his accomplishments or abilities to his own merits.

"but our sufficiency is of God;" - Paul emphasizes that the source of their sufficiency and competence is God Himself. Everything they accomplish in their ministry is by the grace and enabling of God. He acknowledges that their qualifications and effectiveness come from God alone.

This verse emphasizes the humility and dependence of Paul and his co-workers on the divine sufficiency and grace of God. They recognize that they are not self-sufficient but reliant on God's empowerment for their ministry.

Verse 6 (2 Corinthians 3:6, KJV):

"Who also hath made us able ministers of the new testament; not of the letter, but of the spirit: for the letter killeth, but the spirit giveth life."

Expository Commentary on Verse 6:

"Who also hath made us able ministers of the new testament;" - Paul affirms that God has qualified and enabled him and his co-workers to be ministers of the New Covenant. The New Covenant is the era of grace and reconciliation through Christ, in contrast to the Old Covenant based on the Law.

"not of the letter, but of the spirit:" - Paul distinguishes the nature of their ministry from that of the Old Covenant. Their ministry is not based on the letter of the Law but on the Spirit of God. The Old Covenant relied on written laws, while the New Covenant emphasizes the transformative power of the Holy Spirit.

"for the letter killeth, but the spirit giveth life." - Paul contrasts the effects of the Old Covenant (the letter of the Law) with the New Covenant (the ministry of the Spirit). The Old Covenant, which focused on external rules and regulations, had the power to condemn and bring death. In contrast, the New Covenant, empowered by the Spirit, brings life and transformation.

This verse underscores the contrast between the Old Covenant and the New Covenant and highlights the life-giving power of the ministry of the Spirit in the New Covenant era. Paul recognizes that their sufficiency and effectiveness as ministers come from God's enabling through the Holy Spirit.

Verse 7 (2 Corinthians 3:7, KJV):

"But if the ministration of death, written and engraven in stones, was glorious, so that the children of Israel could not steadfastly behold the face of Moses for the glory of his countenance; which glory was to be done away:"

Expository Commentary on Verse 7:

"But if the ministration of death," - Paul begins by referring to the Old Covenant, symbolized by the Ten Commandments, as the "ministration of death." This characterization highlights the condemning nature of the Law. The Law, by revealing sin, pronounced the death sentence on those who could not keep it perfectly.

"written and engraven in stones," - Paul underscores the permanence and authority of the Old Covenant by describing it as written and engraved in stone tablets. The inscribed commandments were set in stone, indicating the unchanging nature of the Law.

"was glorious," - Despite its role as the "ministration of death," the Old Covenant had a certain glory associated with it. This glory was evident in the divine origin and the manner of its revelation.

"so that the children of Israel could not steadfastly behold the face of Moses for the glory of his countenance;" - Paul alludes to the episode in Exodus 34 when Moses descended from Mount Sinai with the second set of stone tablets containing the commandments. His face shone with the glory of God to the extent that the Israelites couldn't bear to look at him directly.

"which glory was to be done away:" - Despite the temporary radiance of Moses' face, it was destined to fade away. The glory associated with the Old Covenant was temporal and would eventually be replaced by the greater glory of the New Covenant.

In this verse, Paul contrasts the Old Covenant with the New Covenant and emphasizes the fading glory of the former in comparison to the enduring and superior glory of the latter.

Verse 8 (2 Corinthians 3:8, KJV):

"How shall not the ministration of the spirit be rather glorious?"

Expository Commentary on Verse 8:

"How shall not the ministration of the spirit be rather glorious?" - Paul introduces a rhetorical question to highlight the superiority of the New Covenant over the Old. He implies that if the Old Covenant, despite its temporary glory, was glorious, then the ministry of the Spirit in the New Covenant is even more glorious.

Paul anticipates that his readers will readily acknowledge the greater glory associated with the New Covenant, which is characterized by the ministry of the Holy Spirit, grace, and the message of salvation through Christ.

Verse 9 (2 Corinthians 3:9, KJV):

"For if the ministration of condemnation be glory, much more doth the ministration of righteousness exceed in glory."

Expository Commentary on Verse 9:

"For if the ministration of condemnation be glory," - Paul continues to contrast the Old and New Covenants. He characterizes the Old Covenant as the "ministration of condemnation" because it revealed and condemned sin. Despite this aspect, it still had glory, as it came from God.

"much more doth the ministration of righteousness exceed in glory." - In comparison, the New Covenant is described as the "ministration of righteousness," signifying the imputed righteousness and justification that comes through faith in Christ. Paul asserts that the glory of the New Covenant surpasses that of the Old Covenant. The righteousness provided through faith in Christ far exceeds the glory of the Law.

Paul's argument emphasizes the surpassing glory of the New Covenant, which offers righteousness and life through faith in Christ, in contrast to the condemnation and death brought by the Old Covenant.

Verse 10 (2 Corinthians 3:10, KJV):

"For even that which was made glorious had no glory in this respect, by reason of the glory that excelleth."

Expository Commentary on Verse 10:

"For even that which was made glorious had no glory in this respect," - Paul reiterates the limited glory of the Old Covenant in comparison to the New Covenant. The Old Covenant's glory was overshadowed by the excellence of the New Covenant.

"by reason of the glory that excelleth." - The glory of the New Covenant surpasses the glory of the Old Covenant. The excellence of the New Covenant, characterized by the ministry of the Spirit and righteousness through Christ, is of a higher order.

Paul underscores the point that the New Covenant's glory so far surpasses the glory of the Old Covenant that the latter seems to have no glory in comparison.

Verse 11 (2 Corinthians 3:11, KJV):

"For if that which is done away was glorious, much more that which remaineth is glorious."

Expository Commentary on Verse 11:

"For if that which is done away was glorious," - Paul reiterates the transient nature of the glory associated with the Old Covenant. It was "done away" or abolished in Christ.

"much more that which remaineth is glorious." - In contrast, the New Covenant, which remains and endures, is characterized by a greater and lasting glory. The glory of the New Covenant is not subject to fading or abolition; it remains glorious and permanent.

This verse reinforces the idea that the New Covenant's glory surpasses that of the Old Covenant because it is characterized by permanence, righteousness, and the indwelling ministry of the Holy Spirit. The Old Covenant served its purpose but was eclipsed by the glory of the New Covenant in Christ.

Verse 12 (2 Corinthians 3:12, KJV):

"Seeing then that we have such hope, we use great plainness of speech:"

Expository Commentary on Verse 12:

"Seeing then that we have such hope," - Paul begins this section by referencing the hope that believers have in Christ. This hope is grounded in the promises of the New Covenant, the ministry of the Spirit, and the surpassing glory of Christ. It's a hope of transformation and eternal life.

"we use great plainness of speech:" - Because of this hope, Paul emphasizes the clarity and simplicity of his communication. He does not resort to obscure or veiled language. Instead, he speaks plainly and openly to make the message of the gospel accessible and understandable to all.

Paul's use of "great plainness of speech" reflects his commitment to clear and straightforward communication, which is a hallmark of effective gospel preaching.

Verse 13 (2 Corinthians 3:13, KJV):

"And not as Moses, which put a veil over his face, that the children of Israel could not steadfastly look to the end of that which is abolished:"

Expository Commentary on Verse 13:

"And not as Moses, which put a veil over his face," - Paul draws a parallel between his ministry and that of Moses. Moses, after receiving the Law on Mount Sinai, veiled his face because it shone with the glory of God. This veil served as a temporary covering to shield the Israelites from the radiance of God's glory.

"that the children of Israel could not steadfastly look to the end of that which is abolished:" - The purpose of the veil was to prevent the Israelites from seeing the fading glory of the Old Covenant. The Old Covenant was destined to be abolished or brought to an end, and the fading glory of Moses' face symbolized the temporary nature of the Law.

Paul uses this historical illustration to make a point about the superior and enduring glory of the New Covenant.

Verse 14 (2 Corinthians 3:14, KJV):

"But their minds were blinded: for until this day remaineth the same veil untaken away in the reading of the old testament; which veil is done away in Christ."

Expository Commentary on Verse 14:

"But their minds were blinded:" - Paul explains that the Israelites' understanding was veiled or obscured. They did not fully comprehend the spiritual significance and fulfillment of the Old Covenant in Christ.

"for until this day remaineth the same veil untaken away in the reading of the old testament;" - Paul highlights that, even in his time, many Jews continued to read the Old Testament with a veil of spiritual blindness. They were unable to see the connection between the Old Covenant and the fulfillment of God's promises in Christ.

"which veil is done away in Christ." - The veil that obscured their understanding is removed in Christ. Through faith in Jesus, the significance and fulfillment of the Old Covenant become clear. Christ is the key to unlocking the spiritual meaning of the Old Testament.

Paul emphasizes the transformation that occurs when people turn to Christ and how He removes the veil that had hindered their understanding of the Old Covenant.

Verse 15 (2 Corinthians 3:15, KJV):

"But even unto this day, when Moses is read, the veil is upon their heart."

Expository Commentary on Verse 15:

"But even unto this day, when Moses is read," - Paul acknowledges that, even in his time, when the writings of Moses (the Old Testament) are read among the Jews, a spiritual veil remains. The veil metaphorically represents their inability to fully grasp the spiritual significance of the Law and the prophetic foreshadowing of Christ in the Old Testament.

"the veil is upon their heart." - The veil is not physical but metaphorical, symbolizing a spiritual condition where the hearts and minds of the Jewish readers remain veiled or covered, preventing them from seeing the fulfillment of the Law in Christ.

Paul highlights the ongoing spiritual blindness that some Jews experience when reading the Old Testament, emphasizing the need for them to turn to Christ for clarity and understanding.

Verse 16 (2 Corinthians 3:16, KJV):

"Nevertheless when it shall turn to the Lord, the veil shall be taken away."

Expository Commentary on Verse 16:

"Nevertheless when it shall turn to the Lord," - Paul offers hope and a condition for the removal of the veil. The veil of spiritual blindness is taken away when an individual or a collective group "turns to the Lord." This means that when one turns to Christ in faith, acknowledging Him as Lord and Savior, the veil is lifted.

"the veil shall be taken away." - When a person turns to the Lord in faith, the spiritual veil that hindered their understanding of the Old Covenant is removed. They gain clarity and insight into the spiritual truths and fulfillment of the Law in Christ.

This verse underscores the transformative power of turning to the Lord in faith. Through faith in Christ, spiritual blindness is replaced with spiritual understanding.

Verse 17 (2 Corinthians 3:17, KJV):

"Now the Lord is that Spirit: and where the Spirit of the Lord is, there is liberty."

Expository Commentary on Verse 17:

"Now the Lord is that Spirit:" - Paul makes a profound declaration, affirming that the Lord (Jesus Christ) is the same as the Spirit. He emphasizes the identity and unity between Christ and the Holy Spirit. The Spirit of God and Christ are one and the same.

"and where the Spirit of the Lord is, there is liberty." - Paul emphasizes that where the Spirit of the Lord is present, there is freedom or liberty. This liberty is spiritual freedom from the bondage of sin and the law. The Holy Spirit brings a sense of freedom and release from the constraints of the Old Covenant.

This verse highlights the role of the Holy Spirit in bringing spiritual freedom and transformation in the lives of believers. In Christ and through the Spirit, believers experience liberation from the power of sin and the old religious systems.

Certainly! Here is an expository study and comprehensive commentary on 2 Corinthians Chapter 3, verse 18, using the King James Bible with references:

Verse 18 (2 Corinthians 3:18, KJV):

"But we all, with open face beholding as in a glass the glory of the Lord, are changed into the same image from glory to glory, even as by the Spirit of the Lord."

Expository Commentary on Verse 18:

In this verse, Paul explores the transformative power of gazing upon the glory of the Lord and the role of the Spirit in this process.

- "But we all," - Paul addresses the collective body of believers, emphasizing that this transformation is not limited to a select few but is available to all Christians.

- "with open face beholding as in a glass the glory of the Lord," - The phrase "open face" means with unveiled faces. Paul draws a parallel between gazing into a mirror or glass and beholding the glory of the Lord. Just as one looks into a mirror to see their own reflection, believers are called to look upon and contemplate the glory of the Lord. This reflection or image of the Lord's glory is made known through the gospel and the revelation of Christ.

- "are changed into the same image from glory to glory," - As believers gaze upon the glory of the Lord, they are transformed into the same image or likeness of Christ. This transformation is ongoing, progressing from one degree of glory to another. It signifies spiritual growth and maturation in the Christian life.

- "even as by the Spirit of the Lord." - The transformative process is attributed to the work of the Spirit of the Lord. The Holy Spirit plays a vital role in changing believers into the likeness of Christ. The Spirit convicts, guides, empowers, and sanctifies, making this transformation possible.

Key Points:

1. Universal Transformation: Paul emphasizes that the transformation into Christ's likeness is available to all believers, making it an inclusive promise for the Christian community.

2. The Role of Contemplation: The act of beholding or contemplating the glory of the Lord is central to this process. It involves focusing on Christ, understanding His character and work, and allowing that knowledge to impact one's life.

3. Progressive Transformation: The transformation is an ongoing journey, moving from one level of glory to the next. This indicates that the Christian life is characterized by growth and maturation.

4. The Holy Spirit's Work: The work of transformation is attributed to the Holy Spirit, highlighting the Spirit's role in the believer's sanctification and spiritual development.

This verse serves as a powerful reminder of the transformative nature of the Christian journey. Believers are encouraged to continually focus on Christ, allowing the Holy Spirit to shape them into His likeness, leading to spiritual growth and maturity. It reflects the idea of becoming more like Christ as a lifelong process guided by the Spirit.

Chapter 4
The Nature of Christian Ministry

The theme of 2 Corinthians Chapter 4 is the nature of Christian ministry, the challenges faced by those who serve in ministry, and the contrast between the earthly and the eternal. In this chapter, the apostle Paul discusses the difficulties and triumphs of the Christian ministry, emphasizing the power and purpose of the gospel message.

Key themes in 2 Corinthians Chapter 4 include:

1. The Treasure in Earthen Vessels: The central theme is the idea that the glory of the gospel is contained in "earthen vessels," referring to the fragility of human bodies. This underscores the notion that the power and significance of the message are from God, not from human strength.

2. Perseverance in Suffering: Paul speaks about the challenges and suffering faced in ministry, emphasizing the importance of perseverance and not losing heart. Despite the difficulties, he is determined to continue proclaiming the gospel.

3. The Light of the Gospel: The chapter highlights the role of the gospel as the light of Christ shining in the hearts of believers. This light dispels darkness and brings the knowledge of God's glory.

4. The Ministry of Reconciliation: Paul discusses the ministry of reconciliation, where believers are called to bring others to God through Christ. He emphasizes that it is God's work and grace that enables this ministry.

5. Eternal Perspective: The chapter emphasizes the contrast between the temporal and the eternal. While outwardly, believers may experience affliction and hardship, inwardly, they are being renewed and are focused on the eternal glory that surpasses all earthly troubles.

6. Renewed Inner Nature: Paul speaks about the inner nature being renewed day by day, which highlights the ongoing transformation and growth in the life of a believer.

In summary, 2 Corinthians Chapter 4 explores the themes of Christian ministry, the challenges and suffering faced by ministers, the power of the gospel, the contrast between the earthly and the eternal, and the renewal of the inner nature. It encourages believers to persevere in their service, understanding that the true source of power and significance is God Himself.

Verse 1 (2 Corinthians 4:1, KJV):

"Therefore, seeing we have this ministry, as we have received mercy, we faint not;"

Expository Commentary on Verse 1:

"Therefore, seeing we have this ministry," - Paul begins this section by referring to the ministry that he and his fellow workers have received. This ministry includes the proclamation of the gospel and the service of spreading the message of Christ.

"as we have received mercy," - Paul emphasizes that their ability to engage in this ministry is an act of God's mercy. They have been entrusted with this responsibility by the grace of God.

"we faint not;" - Despite the challenges and difficulties that come with their ministry, Paul and his companions do not lose heart or become discouraged. They persevere and remain steadfast in their commitment to the task.

In this verse, Paul highlights the significance of the ministry they've received and underscores their resilience and determination in fulfilling it, grounded in the mercy of God.

Verse 2 (2 Corinthians 4:2, KJV):

"But have renounced the hidden things of dishonesty, not walking in craftiness, nor handling the word of God deceitfully, but by manifestation of the truth, commending ourselves to every man's conscience in the sight of God."

Expository Commentary on Verse 2:

"But have renounced the hidden things of dishonesty," - Paul emphasizes the integrity of their ministry. They have turned away from and renounced any form of deceit, dishonesty, or hidden motives. Their approach to ministry is marked by transparency and truthfulness.

"not walking in craftiness," - They do not engage in cunning or deceitful tactics in their ministry. Craftiness refers to the use of clever but deceptive methods.

"nor handling the word of God deceitfully," - Paul underscores their commitment to handling the Word of God, the Scriptures, with honesty and sincerity. They do not manipulate or distort the message for personal gain.

"but by manifestation of the truth," - Instead, they make the truth manifest and clear in their ministry. They seek to present the gospel plainly and honestly.

"commending ourselves to every man's conscience in the sight of God." - Their ministry is characterized by transparency, not hiding anything from the scrutiny of every person's conscience. They seek to live and minister in a way that is pleasing to God and accountable to Him.

This verse highlights the moral and ethical principles that guide their ministry. They are committed to truthfulness, transparency, and sincerity in their handling of the Word of God.

Verse 3 (2 Corinthians 4:3, KJV):

"But if our gospel be hid, it is hid to them that are lost:"

Expository Commentary on Verse 3:

"But if our gospel be hid," - Paul acknowledges that there are circumstances where their message, the gospel, is veiled or hidden.

"it is hid to them that are lost:" - The gospel remains hidden or veiled to those who are spiritually lost or perishing. The message of salvation may not be comprehensible or accepted by those who have not embraced faith in Christ.

This verse underscores the idea that the reception of the gospel is contingent on an individual's spiritual condition. To those who are perishing, the message may remain obscured.

Verse 4 (2 Corinthians 4:4, KJV):

"In whom the god of this world hath blinded the minds of them which believe not, lest the light of the glorious gospel of Christ, who is the image of God, should shine unto them."

Expository Commentary on Verse 4:

"In whom the god of this world hath blinded the minds of them which believe not," - Here, Paul identifies Satan as "the god of this world" who has the power to blind the minds of unbelievers. This spiritual blindness prevents those who do not believe from fully comprehending and accepting the gospel message.

"lest the light of the glorious gospel of Christ, who is the image of God, should shine unto them." - The purpose of this spiritual blindness is to keep unbelievers from seeing and receiving the brilliant and glorious light of the gospel. Christ, who is described as the image of God, is the embodiment of the gospel message.

Paul emphasizes the spiritual warfare that is at play, with Satan seeking to hinder people from receiving the gospel. The gospel message, represented as the light of Christ, is intended to shine and illuminate the hearts and minds of those who believe.

Verse 5 (2 Corinthians 4:5, KJV):

"For we preach not ourselves, but Christ Jesus the Lord; and ourselves your servants for Jesus' sake."

Expository Commentary on Verse 5:

"For we preach not ourselves," - Paul makes it clear that their ministry is not centered on self-promotion or self-glorification. They do not preach themselves as the focus of their message.

"but Christ Jesus the Lord;" - Instead, their preaching centers on Christ Jesus as Lord. He is the central focus and substance of their message. Their purpose is to proclaim Christ's lordship and the gospel message.

"and ourselves your servants for Jesus' sake." - Paul and his companions view themselves as servants or slaves, dedicated to serving the Corinthians for the sake of Jesus. They minister in a spirit of humility and servanthood, seeking the spiritual well-being of others.

This verse underscores the Christ-centered nature of their ministry and their commitment to serving others for the sake of Jesus and His gospel.

Verse 6 (2 Corinthians 4:6, KJV):

"For God, who commanded the light to shine out of darkness, hath shined in our hearts, to give the light of the knowledge of the glory of God in the face of Jesus Christ."

Expository Commentary on Verse 6:

"For God, who commanded the light to shine out of darkness," - Paul draws an analogy between the creative act of God in Genesis, where He commanded light to shine in the darkness, and the spiritual transformation of believers. Just as God brought physical light into the world, He also brings spiritual light to the hearts of believers.

"hath shined in our hearts," - Paul emphasizes that God has personally illuminated their hearts. This divine work is a sovereign act of God, shining His light into the innermost being of believers.

"to give the light of the knowledge of the glory of God in the face of Jesus Christ." - The purpose of this divine illumination is to provide believers with the knowledge of the glorious revelation of God's presence, which is fully realized in the person of Jesus Christ. In beholding Christ, believers gain an understanding of the glory of God.

This verse emphasizes the transformative work of God in the hearts of believers, bringing spiritual illumination and the knowledge of God's glory through Jesus Christ. It highlights the role of divine grace and revelation in the Christian faith.

Verse 7 (2 Corinthians 4:7, KJV):

"But we have this treasure in earthen vessels, that the excellency of the power may be of God, and not of us."

Expository Commentary on Verse 7:

"But we have this treasure in earthen vessels," - Paul uses the metaphor of "earthen vessels" to describe the fragility and imperfection of human beings, including himself and his fellow workers. The "treasure" he refers to is the gospel message and the knowledge of Christ. This treasure is carried by, or entrusted to, imperfect and mortal human vessels.

"that the excellency of the power may be of God, and not of us." - The purpose of entrusting the gospel to these frail and fallible vessels is to highlight that the power and effectiveness of the message do not originate from them but from God. It emphasizes the divine source of the gospel's transformative power and the humility of those who proclaim it.

Paul underscores that the effectiveness of their ministry is not dependent on their abilities or strengths but on the divine power at work in them.

Verse 8 (2 Corinthians 4:8, KJV):

"We are troubled on every side, yet not distressed; we are perplexed, but not in despair;"

Expository Commentary on Verse 8:

"We are troubled on every side, yet not distressed;" - Paul acknowledges that he and his fellow workers face various challenges and difficulties in their ministry. They encounter troubles and adversities from all sides, but despite these, they are not overwhelmed or crushed. The challenges do not lead to despair.

"we are perplexed, but not in despair;" - The term "perplexed" indicates that they may not always understand the reasons or solutions to their challenges. Yet, even in times of perplexity, they do not lose hope or fall into despair. Their faith remains steadfast.

This verse reveals the resilience and endurance of Paul and his companions in the face of adversity. They acknowledge the difficulties but do not lose faith or give in to despair.

Verse 9 (2 Corinthians 4:9, KJV):

"Persecuted, but not forsaken; cast down, but not destroyed;"

Expository Commentary on Verse 9:

"Persecuted, but not forsaken;" - Paul and his fellow workers experience persecution for their faith and ministry. They are targets of hostility and opposition, but they are not abandoned or forsaken by God. His presence sustains them through persecution.

"cast down, but not destroyed;" - They may be brought low or cast down by the challenges and sufferings they face, but they are not ultimately destroyed. Their faith remains intact, and they endure through their difficulties.

This verse underscores the divine preservation and resilience of Paul and his companions in the face of persecution and adversity. They draw strength from their faith and their trust in God's faithfulness.

Verse 10 (2 Corinthians 4:10, KJV):

"Always bearing about in the body the dying of the Lord Jesus, that the life also of Jesus might be made manifest in our body."

Expository Commentary on Verse 10:

"Always bearing about in the body the dying of the Lord Jesus," - Paul reflects on the hardships and suffering they endure in their physical bodies. He uses the language of carrying or bearing the "dying of the Lord Jesus" to express that their sufferings are in some way connected to the sufferings of Christ. They share in His suffering as they serve Him.

"that the life also of Jesus might be made manifest in our body." - The purpose of enduring these hardships is to make evident the life of Jesus in their mortal bodies. Through their suffering and perseverance, the transformative power of Christ's life is displayed and evident to others.

This verse highlights the paradox of Christian suffering, where the trials endured by believers serve as a platform to demonstrate the life and power of Christ.

Verse 11 (2 Corinthians 4:11, KJV):

"For we which live are alway delivered unto death for Jesus' sake, that the life also of Jesus might be made manifest in our mortal flesh."

Expository Commentary on Verse 11:

"For we which live are alway delivered unto death for Jesus' sake," - Paul describes the paradoxical nature of their existence. While they are alive, they continually face the threat of death because of their commitment to Jesus. They are willing to endure hardships, including the risk of physical death, for the sake of their faith and ministry.

"that the life also of Jesus might be made manifest in our mortal flesh." - Just as in the previous verse, the purpose of their suffering and willingness to face death is to display the life of Jesus. This life is evident in their mortal and vulnerable human bodies.

This verse emphasizes the sacrificial nature of their service and their willingness to face adversity and even death for the sake of Christ, with the goal of displaying His life and power through their mortal existence.

Verse 12 (2 Corinthians 4:12, KJV):

"So then death worketh in us, but life in you."

Expository Commentary on Verse 12:

"So then death worketh in us," - In this verse, Paul conveys a profound truth about the nature of his ministry and the sufferings he endures. He describes the experience of "death working in us," which means that he and his fellow workers regularly face trials, hardships, and suffering, even to the point of risking their lives for the sake of the gospel.

This "death" symbolizes the challenges and mortal dangers they confront as they faithfully serve Christ. The apostle Paul himself endured numerous hardships, including beatings, imprisonments, and threats to his life (2 Corinthians 11:23-27).

"but life in you." - In contrast to the suffering and "death" that they experience, Paul emphasizes that their ministry brings life and spiritual transformation to the Corinthians. The trials and sufferings endured by Paul and his companions are not in vain; they serve to bring spiritual life and growth to the Corinthian believers. Through their ministry, the gospel message is proclaimed, faith is nurtured, and people experience the new life in Christ.

This verse underscores the sacrificial nature of Paul's ministry and the transformative power of the gospel. While the ministers may face suffering and challenges, their goal is to bring spiritual life and renewal to those who receive their message. It highlights the paradox of Christian service, where suffering and hardship can lead to spiritual growth and vitality in the lives of believers.

Verse 13 (2 Corinthians 4:13, KJV):

"We having the same spirit of faith, according as it is written, I believed, and therefore have I spoken; we also believe, and therefore speak;"

Expository Commentary on Verse 13:

"We having the same spirit of faith," - Paul begins by emphasizing the shared faith and confidence that he and his fellow workers possess. This "spirit of faith" is a deep and abiding trust in God and His promises. It is the belief that motivates and sustains their ministry.

"according as it is written, I believed, and therefore have I spoken;" - Paul refers to a passage from the Old Testament, likely from Psalm 116:10, where the psalmist expresses his faith by speaking about what he believes. This quote highlights the idea that true faith naturally finds expression in words and actions.

"we also believe, and therefore speak;" - Paul and his companions, like the psalmist, also believe in the truth of the gospel, and this belief compels them to speak boldly about their faith. Their preaching and ministry are an outpouring of their deep-seated faith in Christ.

This verse underscores the connection between genuine faith and verbal confession. True faith results in a spoken testimony and proclamation of one's beliefs, especially in the context of Christian ministry.

Verse 14 (2 Corinthians 4:14, KJV):

"Knowing that he which raised up the Lord Jesus shall raise up us also by Jesus, and shall present us with you."

Expository Commentary on Verse 14:

"Knowing that he which raised up the Lord Jesus shall raise up us also by Jesus," - Paul expresses their confident assurance in the resurrection. They are aware that the same God who raised Jesus from the dead will also raise them, and all believers, to eternal life through the power of Jesus Christ. This knowledge serves as a foundation for their hope and perseverance in the face of trials and suffering.

"and shall present us with you." - Paul anticipates a future reunion when all believers will be presented together. They will be presented before God in a state of glorification and perfected existence. This concept speaks to the ultimate unity and fellowship of believers in the presence of God.

This verse reflects the Christian hope in the resurrection and the future glory that believers will share in Christ. It emphasizes the certainty of resurrection through Jesus and the ultimate presentation of believers before God.

Verse 15 (2 Corinthians 4:15, KJV):

"For all things are for your sakes, that the abundant grace might through the thanksgiving of many redound to the glory of God."

Expository Commentary on Verse 15:

"For all things are for your sakes," - Paul clarifies that everything, including the trials and sufferings they endure, is ultimately for the benefit of the Corinthian believers. Their ministry, hardships, and sacrifices are undertaken for the spiritual growth and well-being of the Corinthians.

"that the abundant grace might through the thanksgiving of many redound to the glory of God." - The purpose of these sacrifices and ministry efforts is to result in an overflowing display of God's grace. When the Corinthians experience the transformative power of the gospel, their gratitude and thanksgiving will be directed toward God. This will, in turn, bring glory to God as others join in giving thanks for His abundant grace.

This verse underscores the selfless and sacrificial nature of Paul's ministry and the ultimate goal of bringing glory to God through the gratitude and transformation of believers. The sufferings and service of the apostle and his companions are all directed towards the spiritual benefit of the Corinthians and the magnification of God's grace.

Verse 16 (2 Corinthians 4:16, KJV):

"For which cause we faint not; but though our outward man perish, yet the inward man is renewed day by day."

Expository Commentary on Verse 16:

"For which cause we faint not;" - Paul begins by affirming their perseverance and determination in their ministry. Despite the difficulties and hardships they encounter, they do not lose heart or become discouraged. The "cause" likely refers to their faith in Christ and their commitment to the gospel.

"but though our outward man perish," - Paul acknowledges the reality of physical decay and mortality. The "outward man" refers to the physical body, which is subject to aging and eventual death. The apostle himself experienced numerous physical hardships during his ministry.

"yet the inward man is renewed day by day." - In contrast to the outward body, the "inward man" refers to the inner or spiritual self. Despite the physical challenges, the inner being of the believer is renewed and strengthened on a daily basis. This renewal comes through their relationship with Christ, the indwelling Holy Spirit, and the Word of God.

This verse highlights the paradox of Christian life, where the physical body may weaken, but the spiritual self is continually refreshed and strengthened through faith and communion with God.

Verse 17 (2 Corinthians 4:17, KJV):

"For our light affliction, which is but for a moment, worketh for us a far more exceeding and eternal weight of glory;"

Expository Commentary on Verse 17:

"For our light affliction," - Paul refers to the trials and sufferings that he and his fellow workers endure as "light affliction." This description may seem paradoxical, as he had experienced significant hardships, but he considers them as relatively minor when compared to the eternal realities of God's promises.

"which is but for a moment," - He emphasizes the temporary nature of these afflictions in the grand scheme of eternity. While suffering may be endured in this life, it is limited in its duration compared to the everlasting future.

"worketh for us a far more exceeding and eternal weight of glory;" - The afflictions and sufferings experienced by believers are not in vain. They serve a purpose, and that purpose is to bring about an abundant and eternal weight of glory. In other words, the difficulties faced in this life prepare and contribute to the incomparable and lasting glory that believers will experience in the presence of God.

This verse highlights the perspective of believers on suffering and hardship. In light of the eternal glory awaiting them, their present trials are seen as temporary and comparatively light.

Verse 18 (2 Corinthians 4:18, KJV):

"While we look not at the things which are seen, but at the things which are not seen: for the things which are seen are temporal; but the things which are not seen are eternal."

Expository Commentary on Verse 18:

"While we look not at the things which are seen," - Paul emphasizes that believers should not fixate on the visible, temporal aspects of life. He encourages them to avoid being preoccupied with the physical world and its transient nature.

"but at the things which are not seen:" - Instead, Paul urges believers to direct their attention to the unseen, spiritual realities. These are the eternal and imperishable aspects of life, including the promises of God, the hope of resurrection, and the future glory that awaits believers.

"for the things which are seen are temporal;" - The visible and tangible aspects of life, such as the physical world and its concerns, are temporary and subject to change and decay.

"but the things which are not seen are eternal." - In contrast, the spiritual and unseen realities, such as faith, hope, and the promises of God, are eternal and enduring. These are the things that truly matter and should capture the focus of believers.

This verse encourages believers to maintain an eternal perspective, recognizing that the unseen spiritual realities have lasting significance, while the visible world is transient and fleeting. It underscores the importance of faith and hope in God's promises as believers navigate the challenges of life.

Chapter 5
The Hope of Eternal Life

The theme of 2 Corinthians Chapter 5 is the hope of eternal life and the ministry of reconciliation through Jesus Christ. This chapter explores the concepts of new creation, the believer's heavenly dwelling, and the work of reconciliation accomplished by Christ.

Key themes in 2 Corinthians Chapter 5 include:

1. Hope of Eternal Life: The central theme is the hope of eternal life that believers have in Christ. The chapter speaks of the desire to be clothed with a heavenly dwelling, emphasizing the eternal nature of life with God.

2. New Creation: Paul discusses the idea of believers being a new creation in Christ. The old has passed away, and all things have become new. This highlights the transformative power of the gospel.

3. Ministry of Reconciliation: The chapter underscores the ministry of reconciliation, wherein believers are called to be ambassadors for Christ. Paul explains that God reconciled the world to Himself through Christ and has entrusted believers with the message of reconciliation.

4. Judgment and Accountability: Paul speaks of the judgment seat of Christ, where believers will be held accountable for their deeds, whether

good or bad. This emphasizes the importance of living in a manner pleasing to God.

5. Motivation for Service: The love of Christ constrains believers and motivates them to live for Him and serve as ambassadors of reconciliation. This theme highlights the transformation of one's motives and desires through faith in Christ.

In summary, 2 Corinthians Chapter 5 focuses on the themes of the hope of eternal life, new creation in Christ, the ministry of reconciliation, and the accountability of believers at the judgment seat of Christ. It encourages believers to live with the assurance of eternal life and to actively engage in the ministry of reconciliation, motivated by the love of Christ.

Verse 1 (2 Corinthians 5:1, KJV):

"For we know that if our earthly house of this tabernacle were dissolved, we have a building of God, an house not made with hands, eternal in the heavens."

Expository Commentary on Verse 1:

"For we know that if our earthly house of this tabernacle were dissolved," - Paul begins by expressing a confident and certain knowledge. He refers to the human body as an "earthly house" or a temporary dwelling place. The term "tabernacle" alludes to the frail and transient nature of our physical bodies. In other words, he acknowledges the mortality and perishable quality of our earthly existence.

"we have a building of God, an house not made with hands, eternal in the heavens." - In contrast to the perishable body, believers possess a spiritual and eternal dwelling provided by God. This "building" or "house not made with hands" refers to the glorified, resurrected body that believers will receive in the heavens. It is an eternal and imperishable existence in the presence of God.

Paul introduces the concept of the resurrection body and emphasizes the hope of a future, heavenly dwelling that far surpasses the limitations of our current earthly bodies.

Verse 2 (2 Corinthians 5:2, KJV):

"For in this we groan, earnestly desiring to be clothed upon with our house which is from heaven:"

Expository Commentary on Verse 2:

"For in this we groan," - Paul acknowledges the reality of human suffering and longing. The groaning represents the trials, tribulations, and limitations experienced in our present earthly bodies. It reflects the deep yearning for a better and eternal state.

"earnestly desiring to be clothed upon with our house which is from heaven:" - Believers eagerly desire to exchange their mortal bodies for the heavenly, eternal bodies promised by God. The phrase "clothed upon" implies a complete transformation, as if putting on a new garment. This heavenly dwelling is seen as a superior and glorious state, and believers long for its fulfillment.

This verse highlights the tension between the present, imperfect state of earthly existence and the earnest desire for the future, heavenly dwelling promised by God.

Verse 3 (2 Corinthians 5:3, KJV):

"If so be that being clothed we shall not be found naked."

Expository Commentary on Verse 3:

"If so be that being clothed we shall not be found naked." - Paul introduces the concern that, upon receiving their heavenly bodies, believers will not be left in a state of spiritual nakedness or vulnerability. The new, glorified bodies are seen as a covering or clothing, ensuring that believers will not be without a suitable dwelling.

This verse underscores the completeness and security that believers will experience when they receive their heavenly bodies. The concern is not about literal nakedness but about being fully equipped for eternal life.

Verse 4 (2 Corinthians 5:4, KJV):

"For we that are in this tabernacle do groan, being burdened: not for that we would be unclothed, but clothed upon, that mortality might be swallowed up of life."

Expository Commentary on Verse 4:

"For we that are in this tabernacle do groan, being burdened:" - Paul reiterates the idea of groaning and acknowledges the burdens and trials that come with our earthly, mortal bodies. The limitations and sufferings of the present life weigh heavily on believers.

"not for that we would be unclothed, but clothed upon," - Paul clarifies that the desire is not merely to be rid of the earthly body (unclothed) but to receive the new, heavenly body (clothed upon). The emphasis is on transformation and the exchange of mortality for immortality.

"that mortality might be swallowed up of life." - The ultimate goal is to have mortality, the state of being subject to death, completely replaced by life. The eternal life provided by God's promises will overwhelm and overcome the mortal condition, leading to eternal existence.

This verse emphasizes that the hope is not for mere escape from the earthly body but for a glorious transformation into a state of eternal life and immortality.

Verse 5 (2 Corinthians 5:5, KJV):

"Now he that hath wrought us for the selfsame thing is God, who also hath given unto us the earnest of the Spirit."

Certainly! Here is an expository study and comprehensive commentary on 2 Corinthians Chapter 5, verse 5, using the King James Bible with references:

Verse 5 (2 Corinthians 5:5, KJV):

"Now he that hath wrought us for the selfsame thing is God, who also hath given unto us the earnest of the Spirit."

Expository Commentary on Verse 5:

In this verse, Paul discusses God's role in shaping and preparing believers for a specific purpose and the significance of the earnest of the Spirit.

- "Now he that hath wrought us for the selfsame thing is God," - Paul begins by acknowledging that it is God who has prepared or "wrought" believers for a specific purpose. The phrase "the selfsame thing" likely refers to the resurrection and the eternal life that believers will experience. In other words, God has shaped and readied believers for their future existence with Him.

- "who also hath given unto us the earnest of the Spirit." - The "earnest" is a down payment or guarantee, often given as a token of assurance in a transaction. Here, Paul refers to the Holy Spirit as the earnest or guarantee given to believers. This indicates that the presence of the Holy Spirit in the lives of believers serves as a pledge, a foretaste, and a guarantee of the future blessings they will receive in God's presence.

Key Points:

1. Divine Preparation: Paul emphasizes that God is the one who prepares believers for their future life with Him. This preparation includes the transformation and sanctification of believers through the work of the Holy Spirit.

2. The Role of the Holy Spirit: The Holy Spirit is given as the earnest or guarantee of future blessings. The presence of the Spirit in the lives of believers assures them of the ultimate fulfillment of God's promises, including eternal life and the resurrection.

3. Future Hope: This verse underscores the confident hope that believers have in God's faithfulness to fulfill His promises. The Holy Spirit's presence serves as a testimony of God's commitment to His people.

4. Assurance of Salvation: The concept of earnest is a significant assurance of salvation in Christian theology, signifying that God's work in the believer's life is a guarantee of the ultimate salvation and eternal life to come.

This verse highlights the pivotal role of God in preparing and assuring believers of their future hope, with the Holy Spirit serving as a down payment or guarantee of the blessings and promises to be fully realized in eternity. It emphasizes the assurance and confidence that believers have in God's faithfulness to fulfill His purposes in their lives.

Verse 6 (2 Corinthians 5:6, KJV):

"Therefore we are always confident, knowing that, whilst we are at home in the body, we are absent from the Lord."

Expository Commentary on Verse 6:

"Therefore we are always confident," - Paul begins by expressing the confidence that he and fellow believers have in their relationship with Christ. This confidence is grounded in their faith and trust in the promises of God.

"knowing that, whilst we are at home in the body," - While they are present in their physical bodies on Earth, they are "at home" in the world. This refers to their temporary residence in this earthly life.

"we are absent from the Lord." - Paul contrasts their earthly presence with their absence from the immediate presence of the Lord. This suggests that their ultimate home and true citizenship are in heaven, and they await the full realization of this reality.

This verse highlights the tension between their present earthly existence and their future hope of being in the direct presence of the Lord. Their confidence is based on the assurance of that future reality.

Verse 7 (2 Corinthians 5:7, KJV):

"(For we walk by faith, not by sight:)"

Expository Commentary on Verse 7:

"(For we walk by faith, not by sight:)" - Paul reinforces the idea that the Christian journey is one guided by faith. Believers do not rely on what they can physically see or experience; rather, their path is defined by trust in the unseen and the promises of God. This principle emphasizes the significance of faith in the Christian life.

This verse underscores the importance of faith as the guiding principle for believers. It means that their trust in God and His promises directs their actions and decisions, even when they cannot perceive them with their physical senses.

Verse 8 (2 Corinthians 5:8, KJV):

"We are confident, I say, and willing rather to be absent from the body, and to be present with the Lord."

Expository Commentary on Verse 8:

"We are confident, I say," - Paul reiterates the confidence that he and other believers possess, especially in the context of their relationship with the Lord.

"and willing rather to be absent from the body, and to be present with the Lord." - Paul expresses his desire to be absent from the physical body, signifying his readiness to leave this earthly existence behind. He longs for the ultimate presence of the Lord in the heavenly realm, highlighting the believer's hope for eternal communion with God.

This verse reflects the Christian's longing for the immediate presence of the Lord, indicating a desire to leave the earthly body and experience the fullness of fellowship with God.

Verse 9 (2 Corinthians 5:9, KJV):

"Wherefore we labour, that, whether present or absent, we may be accepted of him."

Expository Commentary on Verse 9:

"Wherefore we labour," - In response to their hope of being accepted by the Lord, Paul conveys that believers engage in labor or diligent effort. Their labor is directed toward living in a manner that is pleasing to God.

"that, whether present or absent, we may be accepted of him." - The goal of their labor is to be found acceptable to the Lord, whether they are currently present in the body or absent from it. In all circumstances, their aim is to live in a way that is pleasing and acceptable to God.

This verse emphasizes the believer's commitment to a life of holiness and service, motivated by the desire to be pleasing and acceptable to the Lord, regardless of their current state of existence.

Verse 10 (2 Corinthians 5:10, KJV):

"For we must all appear before the judgment seat of Christ; that every one may receive the things done in his body, according to that he hath done, whether it be good or bad."

Expository Commentary on Verse 10:

"For we must all appear before the judgment seat of Christ;" - Paul affirms the universal reality that all believers will stand before the judgment seat of Christ. This is a reference to the future judgment of believers, not for salvation but for the evaluation of their works and actions in this life.

"that every one may receive the things done in his body," - At the judgment seat of Christ, every believer will be evaluated for the deeds and actions performed in their earthly bodies. The emphasis is on what has been accomplished during their earthly lives.

"according to that he hath done, whether it be good or bad." - The judgment will result in a reckoning of one's deeds, whether they are praiseworthy or lacking in virtue. Believers will be rewarded for their good works and actions, while any unfaithful or unworthy deeds will be subject to loss.

This verse highlights the future accountability of believers before Christ's judgment seat. It underscores the importance of a life characterized by good works and faithful service to the Lord.

Verse 11 (2 Corinthians 5:11, KJV):

"Knowing therefore the terror of the Lord, we persuade men; but we are made manifest unto God; and I trust also are made manifest in your consciences."

Expository Commentary on Verse 11:

"Knowing therefore the terror of the Lord, we persuade men;" - Paul begins by acknowledging the awareness of the solemnity and seriousness of the Lord's judgment. He and his fellow workers are conscious of the accountability that all individuals will have before God's judgment seat. This knowledge compels them to persuade or urge people to turn to God, to repent, and to embrace the gospel message.

"but we are made manifest unto God;" - Paul emphasizes that their ministry and motives are fully known and revealed to God. They are transparent and sincere in their service.

"and I trust also are made manifest in your consciences." - Paul believes that their sincerity and integrity are evident not only to God but also to the Corinthians. He trusts that their consciences bear witness to the authenticity of their ministry and their genuine concern for the spiritual well-being of the Corinthians.

This verse underscores the seriousness of the Christian mission and the urgency of persuading others to turn to God, motivated by a profound understanding of God's judgment and accountability.

Verse 12 (2 Corinthians 5:12, KJV):

"For we commend not ourselves again unto you, but give you occasion to glory on our behalf, that ye may have somewhat to answer them which glory in appearance, and not in heart."

Expository Commentary on Verse 12:

"For we commend not ourselves again unto you," - Paul clarifies that he and his companions are not attempting to boast or commend themselves to the Corinthians anew. They do not seek self-promotion or validation from the Corinthians.

"but give you occasion to glory on our behalf," - Instead, their desire is to provide the Corinthians with reasons to take pride in them. They aim to offer the Corinthians legitimate reasons for celebrating and acknowledging their ministry.

"that ye may have somewhat to answer them which glory in appearance, and not in heart." - Paul's purpose is to equip the Corinthians with responses to those who boast superficially, based on outward appearances rather than sincere, heart-felt ministry. He encourages the Corinthians to have a valid and meaningful response to such individuals.

This verse highlights the genuine and unselfish nature of Paul's ministry and his intention to empower the Corinthians to defend the authenticity of their service in contrast to those who rely on outward appearances.

Verse 13 (2 Corinthians 5:13, KJV):

"For whether we be beside ourselves, it is to God: or whether we be sober, it is for your cause."

Expository Commentary on Verse 13:

"For whether we be beside ourselves, it is to God:" - Paul acknowledges that some may perceive him and his fellow workers as being overly zealous or seemingly irrational in their dedication and service to God. However, he clarifies that such extreme devotion is directed toward God, reflecting their fervent commitment to the Lord.

"or whether we be sober, it is for your cause." - On the other hand, when they exhibit self-control and sobriety, it is for the benefit and welfare of the Corinthians. Their actions and demeanor are purposeful and measured, with the Corinthians' well-being in mind.

This verse highlights the balance in Paul's ministry. Whether he appears enthusiastic or composed, his actions are motivated by devotion to God and a genuine concern for the spiritual growth and welfare of the Corinthians.

Verse 14 (2 Corinthians 5:14, KJV):

"For the love of Christ constraineth us; because we thus judge, that if one died for all, then were all dead:"

Expository Commentary on Verse 14:

"For the love of Christ constraineth us;" - Paul identifies the driving force behind their ministry, which is the love of Christ. The profound and sacrificial love of Christ compels and constrains them to serve others and proclaim the gospel.

"because we thus judge," - Their understanding and conviction about the love of Christ lead to their judgment or conclusion.

"that if one died for all, then were all dead:" - Paul's judgment is that if Christ died for all, it indicates that all were spiritually dead in their sins and needed salvation. The death of Christ on the cross was an atonement for the sins of humanity.

This verse underscores the transformative power of Christ's love in motivating believers to serve and share the gospel. It also highlights the foundational understanding that all people, by nature, are spiritually dead and in need of salvation.

Verse 15 (2 Corinthians 5:15, KJV):

"And that he died for all, that they which live should not henceforth live unto themselves, but unto him which died for them, and rose again."

Expository Commentary on Verse 15:

"And that he died for all," - Paul reiterates the central message that Christ died for the sake of all humanity. His sacrifice was not limited to a particular group but had universal significance.

"that they which live should not henceforth live unto themselves," - The purpose of Christ's death is that those who receive new life in Him should no longer live for their own selfish desires and interests. Believers are called to a life of selflessness and devotion to Christ.

"but unto him which died for them, and rose again." - The transformed life of believers is directed towards Christ, who not only died for them but also rose from the dead. This emphasizes the ongoing relationship and devotion to the living Christ who conquered death.

This verse underscores the transformative impact of Christ's death and resurrection on the lives of believers. They are called to live in devotion to Him, no longer for themselves. Their lives are to be characterized by selflessness and allegiance to the risen Savior.

Verse 16 (2 Corinthians 5:16, KJV):

"Wherefore henceforth know we no man after the flesh: yea, though we have known Christ after the flesh, yet now henceforth know we him no more."

Expository Commentary on Verse 16:

"Wherefore henceforth know we no man after the flesh:" - Paul emphasizes a significant transformation in their perspective and relationships. They no longer evaluate, or judge people based on their outward appearances, human status, or worldly standards. This change in outlook is a result of their faith in Christ and the indwelling Holy Spirit.

"Yea, though we have known Christ after the flesh, yet now henceforth know we him no more." - Paul acknowledges that even if they once knew Christ in His physical, earthly form, they no longer know Him in the same way. Their knowledge of Christ has evolved to a spiritual understanding of His divinity and His redemptive work. They recognize the risen and exalted Christ, not merely the historical Jesus.

This verse highlights the transformative power of faith and the change in perspective that believers experience. They no longer judge people based on worldly criteria, and their knowledge of Christ transcends the earthly dimension.

Verse 17 (2 Corinthians 5:17, KJV):

"Therefore, if any man be in Christ, he is a new creature: old things are passed away; behold, all things are become new."

Expository Commentary on Verse 17:

"Therefore, if any man be in Christ, he is a new creature:" - Paul introduces a fundamental truth about the impact of being in Christ. When an individual places their faith in Jesus Christ and becomes a part of Him through faith and regeneration, they experience a radical transformation. They are no longer the same person they once were. This transformation is often referred to as being "born again."

"old things are passed away;" - The old way of life, including the sinful and worldly behaviors and attitudes, has passed away. It is a reference to the former, unregenerate state of the individual.

"Behold, all things are become new." - With the new birth and indwelling of the Holy Spirit, a profound change takes place in the person's life. Their thoughts, desires, values, and actions are renewed and transformed according to the righteousness and holiness of Christ.

This verse emphasizes the transformative nature of the Christian experience. Those who are in Christ become new creations, with their old, sinful nature being replaced by a new, godly nature.

Verse 18 (2 Corinthians 5:18, KJV):

"And all things are of God, who hath reconciled us to himself by Jesus Christ, and hath given to us the ministry of reconciliation;"

Expository Commentary on Verse 18:

"And all things are of God," - Paul affirms that the entire process of reconciliation and transformation is initiated and accomplished by God. It is a divine work from start to finish.

"who hath reconciled us to himself by Jesus Christ," - The central focus is on reconciliation. Through Jesus Christ, God has brought about reconciliation between Himself and humanity. This reconciliation is made possible through the atoning work of Christ on the cross.

"and hath given to us the ministry of reconciliation;" - God not only reconciled believers to Himself but also entrusted them with the ministry of reconciliation. Believers are commissioned to proclaim the message of reconciliation to others, inviting them to be reconciled to God through faith in Christ.

This verse highlights the divine origin of reconciliation and emphasizes the role of believers in sharing this message with the world.

Verse 19 (2 Corinthians 5:19, KJV):

"To wit, that God was in Christ, reconciling the world unto himself, not imputing their trespasses unto them; and hath committed unto us the word of reconciliation."

Expository Commentary on Verse 19:

"To wit, that God was in Christ, reconciling the world unto himself," - Paul elaborates on the process of reconciliation. He explains that God was fully present in Christ, working to bring about reconciliation between Himself and the world. This reconciliation involves the removal of the barrier of sin that separated humanity from God.

"not imputing their trespasses unto them;" - As part of the reconciliation process, God does not hold humanity's sins against them. Instead, He offers forgiveness and grace, demonstrating His mercy and love.

"and hath committed unto us the word of reconciliation." - Believers have been entrusted with the message of reconciliation. It is their responsibility to share the gospel, proclaiming the good news that God has made a way for humanity to be reconciled to Him through Christ.

This verse emphasizes the completeness of God's work in Christ for reconciliation and underscores the role of believers in sharing the message of reconciliation with others.

Verse 20 (2 Corinthians 5:20, KJV):

"Now then we are ambassadors for Christ, as though God did beseech you by us: we pray you in Christ's stead, be ye reconciled to God."

Expository Commentary on Verse 20:

"Now then we are ambassadors for Christ," - Paul and his fellow workers are described as ambassadors representing Christ. They function as messengers and representatives of Christ's kingdom, conveying His message and mission.

"as though God did beseech you by us:" - In their role as ambassadors, it is as if God Himself is making a heartfelt plea or appeal to the Corinthians through the ministry of Paul and his companions.

"we pray you in Christ's stead, be ye reconciled to God." - The appeal is that the Corinthians would embrace reconciliation with God. The ministry of Paul and others is a plea for them to accept God's offer of reconciliation through faith in Christ.

This verse underscores the crucial role of believers as ambassadors, representing Christ and imploring others to be reconciled to God through faith in Christ.

Verse 21 (2 Corinthians 5:21, KJV):

"For he hath made him to be sin for us, who knew no sin; that we might be made the righteousness of God in him."

Expository Commentary on Verse 21:

"For he hath made him to be sin for us," - This verse speaks of the profound exchange that took place on the cross. God the Father made Jesus, who knew no sin, to be sin on behalf of humanity. In other words, Jesus bore the sins of humanity, becoming a sin offering and a substitutionary sacrifice.

"who knew no sin;" - This phrase emphasizes the sinlessness and purity of Jesus. He was completely without sin.

"that we might be made the righteousness of God in him." - The purpose of Christ's substitutionary sacrifice was to enable believers to be clothed in the righteousness of God. Through faith in Christ, believers are counted as righteous before God, not based on their own merit but on the righteousness of Christ imputed to them.

This verse encapsulates the heart of the gospel message, highlighting the atonement and imputed righteousness made possible through Christ's sacrificial death on the cross. Believers are declared righteous in Christ, while He took upon Himself the burden of their sins.

Chapter 6
The Call to Holiness

The theme of 2 Corinthians Chapter 6 is the call to holiness, separation from worldly influences, and the ministry of reconciliation. In this chapter, the apostle Paul emphasizes the importance of living in a manner that is pleasing to God and highlights the challenges and responsibilities of Christian ministry.

Key themes in 2 Corinthians Chapter 6 include:

1. Ministry of Reconciliation: The central theme is the ministry of reconciliation. Paul describes the work of ministry as a partnership with God in reconciling people to Him through the message of Christ.

2. Urgency and Acceptable Time: Paul underscores the urgency of the message and the importance of responding to God's grace in a timely manner. He quotes from the book of Isaiah, calling the present time "the acceptable time" for salvation.

3. Holiness and Separation: The chapter emphasizes the call to holiness and separation from worldly influences. Paul encourages believers to live pure, blameless lives and avoid entanglements with unbelievers.

4. Suffering and Perseverance: Paul acknowledges the challenges and hardships faced in ministry, including tribulations, distress, and persecution. He highlights the importance of perseverance and enduring trials for the sake of the gospel.

5. Unity and Affection: Despite the trials and challenges, Paul expresses his affection for the Corinthians and desires a reciprocal outpouring of love from them.

6. Open Hearts and Reciprocal Love: Paul encourages the Corinthians to open their hearts to him and receive his ministry. He desires mutual affection and appreciation.

In summary, 2 Corinthians Chapter 6 underscores the themes of the ministry of reconciliation, holiness, separation from worldly influences, and the challenges and responsibilities of Christian ministry. It encourages believers to live in a manner that is pleasing to God, to embrace the message of Christ, and to participate in the ministry of reconciliation, while also highlighting the importance of enduring hardships and challenges for the sake of the gospel.

Verse 1 (2 Corinthians 6:1, KJV):

"We then, as workers together with him, beseech you also that ye receive not the grace of God in vain."

Expository Commentary on Verse 1:

"We then, as workers together with him," - In this verse, Paul is referring to himself, his fellow workers, and all believers as co-laborers or fellow workers with God. This implies that they are actively engaged in God's mission, partnering with Him to fulfill His purposes.

"beseech you also that ye receive not the grace of God in vain." - Paul and his co-workers make an earnest plea to the Corinthians. They urge the Corinthians not to receive God's grace in a manner that renders it ineffective or wasted. In essence, they are cautioning against a superficial or fruitless response to the gospel.

This verse emphasizes the cooperative nature of Christian ministry and the importance of responding to God's grace in a way that bears fruit and leads to transformation.

Verse 2 (2 Corinthians 6:2, KJV):

"(For he saith, I have heard thee in a time accepted, and in the day of salvation have I succoured thee: behold, now is the accepted time; behold, now is the day of salvation.)"

Expository Commentary on Verse 2:

"(For he saith, I have heard thee in a time accepted, and in the day of salvation have I succoured thee:" - In this verse, Paul quotes from the Old Testament (Isaiah 49:8) to reinforce his point. The passage in Isaiah speaks of God's response to the cry of the afflicted and the promise of salvation. It signifies that there is a specific, favorable time when God is ready to provide salvation and help.

"behold, now is the accepted time; behold, now is the day of salvation.)" - Paul underscores the urgency of the moment. He emphasizes that the time for receiving God's salvation and grace is now. There is a sense of immediacy and a call to respond to God's offer of salvation without delay.

This verse stresses the importance of seizing the present moment to accept God's grace and salvation. It highlights the sense of urgency in responding to the gospel and emphasizes the need to embrace God's salvation without hesitation.

Verse 3 (2 Corinthians 6:3, KJV):

"Giving no offence in any thing, that the ministry be not blamed:"

Expository Commentary on Verse 3:

"Giving no offence in any thing," - Paul instructs believers to be diligent in living a life that does not cause others to stumble or be offended. They should strive to avoid any actions or behaviors that might hinder the effectiveness of their ministry or tarnish their Christian testimony.

"that the ministry be not blamed:" - The purpose of living a blameless life is to protect the reputation of the Christian ministry. Scandals or offenses can bring disrepute to the work of God, making it less effective and causing people to doubt the sincerity of the message.

This verse underscores the importance of living a life consistent with one's faith to maintain the credibility and impact of the Christian ministry.

Verse 4 (2 Corinthians 6:4, KJV):

"But in all things approving ourselves as the ministers of God, in much patience, in afflictions, in necessities, in distresses,"

Expository Commentary on Verse 4:

"But in all things approving ourselves as the ministers of God," - Paul emphasizes the need for ministers of God to demonstrate their authenticity and sincerity in all aspects of life. They should provide evidence that they are true servants of God, genuinely dedicated to their ministry.

"in much patience," - Patience is a key virtue for those in ministry. It involves enduring trials and hardships with a steadfast and patient spirit, not being easily discouraged.

"in afflictions," - Ministers may experience various forms of suffering, and their ability to endure and remain faithful in the midst of afflictions is a mark of their ministry.

"in necessities," - Necessities refer to times when ministers face significant needs, whether material, emotional, or spiritual. Their reliance on God in such situations demonstrates their trust and dependence on Him.

"in distresses," - Distresses represent situations of extreme difficulty and anguish. Ministers are called to navigate these challenges with faith and reliance on God.

This verse highlights the qualities and experiences that demonstrate the authenticity of one's ministry and the challenges that ministers may face.

Verse 5 (2 Corinthians 6:5, KJV):

"In stripes, in imprisonments, in tumults, in labours, in watchings, in fastings;"

Expository Commentary on Verse 5:

Paul provides a list of specific challenges and experiences faced by ministers in the course of their service:

"In stripes," - This refers to physical beatings or floggings that some ministers endured for their faith and proclamation of the gospel.

"in imprisonments," - Some ministers found themselves imprisoned or detained due to their Christian activities or the hostility of others.

"in tumults," - Tumults indicate times of unrest, disorder, or upheaval. Ministers sometimes had to navigate situations of chaos and upheaval.

"in labours," - The labor and toil associated with ministry, including preaching, teaching, and serving the needs of others.

"in watchings," - Watchings imply periods of sleeplessness or vigilance, often associated with prayer, ministry responsibilities, or persecution.

"in fastings;" - Ministers may engage in voluntary fasts as part of their spiritual disciplines or to seek God's guidance.

This verse highlights the wide range of challenges and hardships that ministers of the gospel may encounter as they faithfully serve God.

Verse 6 (2 Corinthians 6:6, KJV):

"By pureness, by knowledge, by longsuffering, by kindness, by the Holy Ghost, by love unfeigned,"

Expository Commentary on Verse 6:

Paul contrasts the challenges faced in the previous verse with the virtues and qualities that sustain ministers in their service:

"By pureness," - Ministers are to exhibit purity in their character and conduct, maintaining integrity and moral uprightness.

"by knowledge," - Knowledge is essential for effective ministry, enabling ministers to teach and guide others in the truth.

"by longsuffering," - Longsuffering involves patience and endurance in the face of challenges and difficulties.

"by kindness," - Kindness is a disposition of compassion and care for others, a crucial aspect of Christian ministry.

"by the Holy Ghost," - The presence and empowerment of the Holy Spirit are indispensable for effective ministry, providing guidance, wisdom, and spiritual gifts.

"by love unfeigned," - Love, genuine and sincere, is at the heart of ministry. Ministers are to love others without hypocrisy or pretense.

This verse emphasizes the importance of character, virtue, and the presence of the Holy Spirit in the lives of ministers.

Verse 7 (2 Corinthians 6:7, KJV):

"By the word of truth, by the power of God, by the armour of righteousness on the right hand and on the left,"

Expository Commentary on Verse 7:

Paul continues to describe the resources and qualities that enable effective ministry:

"By the word of truth," - Ministers rely on the truth of God's Word to proclaim the gospel and guide believers in the right path.

"by the power of God," - The power of God is the supernatural enablement that equips ministers to perform signs, wonders, and to bring about transformation in people's lives.

"by the armor of righteousness on the right hand and on the left," - The armor of righteousness is a symbol of moral integrity and spiritual readiness. It is to be worn on both sides, signifying comprehensive protection and preparedness for spiritual warfare and challenges.

This verse underscores the spiritual resources and divine enablement that empower ministers in their service and emphasizes the importance of truth, righteousness, and reliance on God's power.

Verse 8 (2 Corinthians 6:8, KJV):

"By honour and dishonour, by evil report and good report: as deceivers, and yet true;"

Expository Commentary on Verse 8:

Paul lists contrasting experiences and perceptions that ministers may encounter:

"By honour and dishonour," - Ministers may experience both honor and dishonor from various people and in different circumstances.

"by evil report and good report:" - They may receive negative reports or accusations as well as positive commendations.

"as deceivers, and yet true;" - Some may accuse ministers of being deceptive, while, in reality, they remain truthful and genuine in their ministry.

This verse acknowledges the paradoxes and conflicting perceptions that ministers often face in the course of their service.

Verse 9 (2 Corinthians 6:9, KJV):

"As unknown, and yet well known; as dying, and, behold, we live; as chastened, and not killed;"

Expository Commentary on Verse 9:

Paul continues to describe the contrasting experiences and paradoxes that ministers may encounter:

"As unknown, and yet well known;" - Ministers may be relatively unknown to some, while being well known and recognized by others.

"as dying, and, behold,

we live;" - They may face circumstances and challenges that appear life-threatening, yet they continue to live and persevere.

"as chastened, and not killed;" - Ministers may undergo discipline or correction, but it does not result in their destruction. They endure and remain effective in their service.

This verse underscores the complex and contrasting experiences that ministers may encounter, highlighting their resilience and faithfulness.

Verse 10 (2 Corinthians 6:10, KJV):

"As sorrowful, yet alway rejoicing; as poor, yet making many rich; as having nothing, and yet possessing all things."

Expository Commentary on Verse 10:

Paul concludes this section by presenting more paradoxical experiences of ministers:

"As sorrowful, yet alway rejoicing;" - Ministers may experience moments of sorrow and distress, yet they maintain a sense of ongoing joy and rejoicing, grounded in their faith.

"as poor, yet making many rich;" - They may have limited material resources, yet they enrich the lives of others through their ministry.

"as having nothing, and yet possessing all things." - In terms of worldly possessions, they may appear to have nothing, yet in the spiritual realm, they possess the riches of God's grace, wisdom, and blessings.

This verse highlights the ability of ministers to navigate contrasting experiences with resilience, joy, and the abundance of spiritual treasures. It reflects the divine paradoxes of Christian service.

Verse 11 (2 Corinthians 6:11, KJV):

"O ye Corinthians, our mouth is open unto you, our heart is enlarged."

Expository Commentary on Verse 11:

"O ye Corinthians," - Paul addresses the Corinthians directly, expressing his concern and affection for them.

"our mouth is open unto you," - Paul emphasizes that he and his fellow workers have been transparent and open in their communication with the Corinthians. They have freely shared the gospel, teachings, and counsel.

"our heart is enlarged." - This phrase reveals the depth of Paul's emotional attachment to the Corinthians. His heart has expanded in love and concern for them. It signifies his genuine care for their well-being and spiritual growth.

This verse highlights the genuine and open-hearted approach of Paul and his co-workers in their relationship with the Corinthians. It reflects the depth of their emotional investment in the Corinthian church.

Verse 12 (2 Corinthians 6:12, KJV):

"Ye are not straitened in us, but ye are straitened in your own bowels."

Expository Commentary on Verse 12:

"Ye are not straitened in us," - Paul reassures the Corinthians that they have not limited or restricted him and his companions in their affection and care for the Corinthians. The Corinthians have not constrained the love and concern that Paul has for them.

"but ye are straitened in your own bowels." - Instead, the Corinthians seem to have constricted or restricted their own hearts or affections. It implies that their response to Paul and his ministry has not been as open or affectionate as it could be. They have limited their own expressions of love and concern.

This verse suggests a desire for the Corinthians to reciprocate the love and concern that Paul and his companions have shown them. It highlights the need for open-hearted and affectionate relationships within the Corinthian church.

Verse 13 (2 Corinthians 6:13, KJV):

"Now for a recompence in the same, (I speak as unto my children,) be ye also enlarged."

Expository Commentary on Verse 13:

"Now for a recompence in the same," - Paul encourages the Corinthians to respond in kind, to reciprocate the love and affection that he has shown them. He desires a mutual exchange of care and concern.

"(I speak as unto my children,)" - Paul's tone is paternal and nurturing, as he regards the Corinthians as his spiritual children. He is guiding them with a fatherly heart.

"be ye also enlarged." - The Corinthians are urged to expand their hearts and affections in response. They should not be constrained but should open themselves to deeper relationships and greater expressions of love and care.

This verse underscores the importance of reciprocal love and affection within the Christian community. Paul encourages the Corinthians to respond to his love by opening their hearts and showing affection in return.

Verse 14 (2 Corinthians 6:14, KJV):

"Be ye not unequally yoked together with unbelievers: for what fellowship hath righteousness with unrighteousness? and what communion hath light with darkness?"

Expository Commentary on Verse 14:

"Be ye not unequally yoked together with unbelievers:" - Paul begins by giving a clear and direct exhortation to the Corinthians. He advises them not to form close, binding relationships or partnerships with those who do not share their faith. The metaphor of being unequally yoked refers to a mismatch or an unequal partnership.

"for what fellowship hath righteousness with unrighteousness?" - Paul highlights the fundamental disparity between the righteous, who are in Christ, and the unrighteous, who are outside of Christ. The two groups have different standards, values, and motivations, making deep fellowship and partnership challenging.

"and what communion hath light with darkness?" - Paul further illustrates the contrast between believers (light) and unbelievers (darkness). Light and darkness represent opposing spiritual conditions, and there is an inherent incompatibility between the two.

This verse emphasizes the importance of maintaining spiritual integrity and not compromising one's faith by forming close associations with unbelievers who may lead them away from their Christian convictions.

Verse 15 (2 Corinthians 6:15, KJV):

"And what concord hath Christ with Belial? or what part hath he that believeth with an infidel?"

Expository Commentary on Verse 15:

"And what concord hath Christ with Belial?" - Paul continues to emphasize the incompatibility of believers and unbelievers by highlighting the vast difference between Christ and Belial. Christ represents the embodiment of righteousness and holiness, while Belial is often associated with wickedness or Satan. The two have nothing in common.

"or what part hath he that believeth with an infidel?" - Paul contrasts the believer with an infidel, emphasizing the divide between faith and unbelief. Those who have faith in Christ are fundamentally different from those who reject Him.

This verse underscores the profound differences between believers and unbelievers, as well as the incompatibility of their respective natures and values.

Verse 16 (2 Corinthians 6:16, KJV):

"And what agreement hath the temple of God with idols? for ye are the temple of the living God; as God hath said, I will dwell in them, and walk in them; and I will be their God, and they shall be my people."

Expository Commentary on Verse 16:

"And what agreement hath the temple of God with idols?" - Paul introduces the metaphor of the temple to further illustrate the incongruity of believers being entangled with unbelievers. The temple of God, representing the presence of God and His holiness, cannot coexist with idols, which symbolize false gods and ungodliness.

"for ye are the temple of the living God;" - Paul reminds the Corinthians of their identity as the temple of the living God. In the New

Testament, believers, collectively and individually, are described as the dwelling place of God through the indwelling of the Holy Spirit.

"as God hath said, I will dwell in them, and walk in them; and I will be their God, and they shall be my people." - Paul quotes from the Old Testament, particularly Leviticus 26:12 and Ezekiel 37:27, to affirm God's promise to dwell among His people and have a close, covenantal relationship with them. Believers are called to be a living testament to this divine indwelling.

This verse emphasizes the holiness and purity of believers as the dwelling place of God and reinforces the incompatibility of such a status with any form of idolatry or ungodliness.

Verse 17 (2 Corinthians 6:17, KJV):

"Wherefore come out from among them, and be ye separate, saith the Lord, and touch not the unclean thing; and I will receive you,"

Expository Commentary on Verse 17:

"Wherefore come out from among them, and be ye separate, saith the Lord," - Building on the previous verses, Paul quotes a command from the Lord to highlight the need for believers to separate themselves from the influence and practices of unbelievers. This separation is not physical isolation but rather a separation in terms of lifestyle, values, and associations.

"and touch not the unclean thing;" - Believers are called to avoid involvement with anything that is considered unclean or defiling. This includes sinful practices, ungodly influences, and any form of moral impurity.

"and I will receive you," - God promises that if believers heed this call to separation and holiness, He will welcome them and have a close relationship with them. This reflects the idea of divine acceptance and intimacy.

This verse underscores the call for believers to maintain a distinct and holy way of life, marked by separation from worldly influences, in order to enjoy a deeper fellowship with God.

Verse 18 (2 Corinthians 6:18, KJV):

"And will be a Father unto you, and ye shall be my sons and daughters, saith the Lord Almighty."

Expository Commentary on Verse 18:

"And will be a Father unto you," - In response to believers' obedience to the call for separation and holiness, God promises to be a Father to them. This signifies a close, intimate, and paternal relationship with believers, marked by care and provision.

"and ye shall be my sons and daughters," - Believers are not only recipients of God's love and care but also His sons and daughters. This language emphasizes the familial, loving, and covenantal nature of their relationship with God.

"saith the Lord Almighty." - God, identified as the Lord Almighty, affirms the certainty and authority of His promises. His power and sovereignty underscore the assurance of the relationship described.

This verse reinforces the idea that living a separated, holy life in obedience to God's call results in a profound and intimate relationship with God as Father and His children. It reflects the rich blessings of divine adoption and covenantal belonging.

Chapter 7
Reconciliation and Repentance

The theme of 2 Corinthians Chapter 7 is reconciliation and repentance, with a focus on the positive outcome of godly sorrow and the joy that comes from restoration and renewed relationships. In this chapter, the apostle Paul discusses the Corinthians' response to his previous letter and their genuine repentance and reconciliation.

Key themes in 2 Corinthians Chapter 7 include:

1. Repentance and Godly Sorrow: The central theme is the concept of godly sorrow and genuine repentance. Paul rejoices that the Corinthians responded to his previous letter with a sense of godly sorrow, which led to a change in their behavior and attitudes.

2. Reconciliation and Restoration: The chapter emphasizes the idea of reconciliation and restoration of broken relationships. Paul expresses his joy in the Corinthians' renewed affection for him and their obedience to his teachings.

3. Comfort in Affliction: Paul discusses the comfort he experienced in the midst of affliction, both from the Corinthians' response and from Titus, who brought him good news about the church's repentance.

4. Contrast with Worldly Sorrow: Paul distinguishes godly sorrow from worldly sorrow. While worldly sorrow leads to death, godly sorrow

leads to repentance and life. He encourages believers to seek the transformative power of godly sorrow.

5. Affection and Joy: The chapter is filled with expressions of affection and joy. Paul has affection for the Corinthians, and he rejoices in their response to his admonishments.

In summary, 2 Corinthians Chapter 7 revolves around the themes of repentance, reconciliation, and the transformative power of godly sorrow. It highlights the positive outcome of a change of heart, leading to the restoration of relationships and the joy that comes from genuine repentance and obedience to God's Word.

Verse 1 (2 Corinthians 7:1, KJV):

"Having therefore these promises, dearly beloved, let us cleanse ourselves from all filthiness of the flesh and spirit, perfecting holiness in the fear of God."

Expository Commentary on Verse 1:

"Having therefore these promises," - Paul begins this verse by referring to the promises that he has alluded to in previous passages. These promises likely include the promise of God's presence and relationship, as mentioned in the preceding chapter, and other promises related to the blessings and benefits of being in Christ.

"dearly beloved," - Paul affectionately addresses the Corinthians as dearly beloved. This term of endearment reflects his deep care and affection for them, despite the challenges he has addressed in his letters.

"let us cleanse ourselves from all filthiness of the flesh and spirit," - In light of the promises and their status as beloved by God, Paul calls on the Corinthians to engage in an ongoing process of spiritual purification. This involves cleansing both the physical and spiritual aspects of their lives. Filthiness of the flesh refers to immoral and impure actions, while filthiness of the spirit encompasses sinful attitudes and thoughts.

"perfecting holiness in the fear of God." - The goal of this cleansing process is to achieve and mature in holiness. Believers are to pursue holiness as a way of life, growing in their separation from sin and conformity to God's moral standards. The fear of God, which is a reverential awe and respect for God's holiness and authority, is the driving force behind this pursuit of holiness.

This verse encourages believers to actively participate in the sanctification process, striving for purity and holiness in their lives, motivated by their love for God and their reverence for His holiness. It reminds them that their conduct should align with the promises of God and their identity as His beloved children.

Verse 2 (2 Corinthians 7:2, KJV):

"Receive us; we have wronged no man, we have corrupted no man, we have defrauded no man."

Expository Commentary on Verse 2:

In this verse, Paul makes a plea to the Corinthians, affirming his integrity and that of his fellow workers. He emphasizes that they have not wronged, corrupted, or defrauded anyone.

- "Receive us;" - Paul is asking the Corinthians to welcome him and his companions. This request may be in response to tensions or doubts that had arisen in their relationship.

- "we have wronged no man," - Paul asserts that he and his co-workers have not committed any injustices or wrongs against anyone. This statement reflects their commitment to living in an upright and just manner.

- "we have corrupted no man," - Paul affirms that they have not led anyone into moral corruption or depravity. Their message and conduct have been morally upright.

- "we have defrauded no man." - Paul claims that they have not engaged in dishonest or fraudulent behavior toward anyone. They have acted with integrity in their dealings.

This verse underscores Paul's commitment to maintaining an upright and blameless reputation in his ministry and relationships.

Verse 3 (2 Corinthians 7:3, KJV):

"I speak not this to condemn you: for I have said before, that ye are in our hearts to die and live with you."

Expository Commentary on Verse 3:

In this verse, Paul clarifies his intentions, assuring the Corinthians that he is not seeking to condemn or accuse them. Instead, he expresses the depth of his affection for them.

- "I speak not this to condemn you:" - Paul wants to make it clear that his previous statement about their integrity is not meant to condemn or criticize the Corinthians. His aim is not to accuse them.

- "for I have said before," - Paul alludes to a previous communication, likely his earlier letter (1 Corinthians), in which he had addressed similar issues and expressed his love for them.

- "that ye are in our hearts to die and live with you." - Paul reveals the profound love and commitment he has for the Corinthians. He is willing to share in their lives' experiences, joys, and challenges. His heart is deeply invested in their well-being.

This verse emphasizes Paul's genuine love and concern for the Corinthians, highlighting his desire for a healthy and loving relationship with them.

Verse 4 (2 Corinthians 7:4, KJV):

"Great is my boldness of speech toward you, great is my glorying of you: I am filled with comfort, I am exceeding joyful in all our tribulation."

Expository Commentary on Verse 4:

In this verse, Paul further expresses his emotions and feelings regarding his relationship with the Corinthians.

- "Great is my boldness of speech toward you," - Paul acknowledges that he is not timid or reserved in his communication with the Corinthians. He is straightforward and open in his speech when addressing them.

- "great is my glorying of you:" - Paul takes pride in the Corinthians and often speaks highly of them. He sees their potential and is encouraged by their growth and progress.

- "I am filled with comfort," - Despite the challenges and issues he addresses, Paul finds comfort and encouragement in his relationship with the Corinthians. Their progress and faith provide him with solace.

- "I am exceeding joyful in all our tribulation." - Even in the midst of trials and hardships, Paul finds exceeding joy. The Corinthians' response to his teaching and their faith in Christ bring him great joy and encouragement.

This verse reflects the complex range of emotions that Paul experiences in his relationship with the Corinthians. It underscores his pride in them, his comfort in their growth, and his joy in the face of tribulations.

Verse 5 (2 Corinthians 7:5, KJV):

"For, when we were come into Macedonia, our flesh had no rest, but we were troubled on every side; without were fightings, within were fears."

Expository Commentary on Verse 5:

In this verse, Paul provides insight into the challenging circumstances he and his companions faced when they arrived in Macedonia.

- "For, when we were come into Macedonia," - Paul begins by explaining the timing of these events. He references their arrival in Macedonia, indicating that the difficulties he describes took place during this period.

- "our flesh had no rest," - Paul uses the phrase "our flesh" to refer to their physical and emotional state. He emphasizes that they found no rest or relief during this time. They were weary and burdened.

- "but we were troubled on every side;" - The apostle describes the external pressures and troubles they encountered. It seemed as though challenges and difficulties were all around them.

- "without were fightings," - Paul mentions external conflicts and struggles, perhaps with adversaries or opposition to their ministry.

- "within were fears." - Internally, Paul and his companions grappled with fears and anxieties. Despite their commitment to their ministry, they were not immune to the human experience of fear and uncertainty.

This verse gives a glimpse into the hardships and pressures faced by Paul and his team during their time in Macedonia, illustrating the human aspects of their missionary journey.

Verse 6 (2 Corinthians 7:6, KJV):

"Nevertheless God, that comforteth those that are cast down, comforted us by the coming of Titus;"

Expository Commentary on Verse 6:

In this verse, Paul shifts his focus to the comforting presence of God and the arrival of Titus.

- "Nevertheless God, that comforteth those that are cast down," - Paul emphasizes the role of God as the source of comfort for those who are in distress or despondent. Despite the challenges they faced, God provided solace and encouragement.

- "comforted us by the coming of Titus;" - Paul highlights the specific means by which God brought comfort to them: the arrival of Titus. Titus, a trusted co-worker and messenger, brought good news and comfort to Paul and his companions.

This verse underscores the divine comfort that sustains believers during times of distress and the significant role of supportive fellow believers like Titus.

Verse 7 (2 Corinthians 7:7, KJV):

"And not by his coming only, but by the consolation wherewith he was comforted in you, when he told us your earnest desire, your mourning, your fervent mind toward me; so that I rejoiced the more."

Expository Commentary on Verse 7:

Paul continues to elaborate on the role of Titus in bringing comfort to him and his companions.

- "And not by his coming only," - Paul clarifies that Titus' presence alone was not the sole source of comfort. It was not merely the fact that Titus had arrived but what he brought with him.

- "but by the consolation wherewith he was comforted in you," - Titus had experienced consolation or comfort among the Corinthians. He found solace in their response to Paul's message.

- "when he told us your earnest desire, your mourning, your fervent mind toward me;" - Titus conveyed to Paul the Corinthians' deep and earnest desires, their mourning, and their passionate concern for Paul. Their response demonstrated their love and support for him.

- "so that I rejoiced the more." - Paul's reaction to Titus' report was one of increased joy. He was overjoyed by the Corinthians' positive response and their affirmation of their affection for him.

This verse highlights the role of Titus as a messenger of good news and comfort, as well as the Corinthians' genuine and heartfelt response to Paul's ministry. Their love and concern brought great joy to Paul.

Verse 8 (2 Corinthians 7:8, KJV):

"For though I made you sorry with a letter, I do not repent, though I did repent for I perceive that the same epistle hath made you sorry, though it were but for a season."

Expository Commentary on Verse 8:

In this verse, Paul discusses the impact of a previous letter he wrote to the Corinthians, which had caused them sorrow.

- "For though I made you sorry with a letter," - Paul acknowledges that a previous letter he sent to the Corinthians had indeed caused them sorrow. He had addressed issues and concerns in that letter, leading to some emotional distress among the Corinthians.

- "I do not repent, though I did repent:" - Here, Paul uses a bit of wordplay to explain his emotions. He initially regretted the sorrow his letter had caused, but he no longer regretted it because he realized the positive outcome it had produced.

- "for I perceive that the same epistle hath made you sorry, though it were but for a season." - Paul recognizes that the sorrow induced by the letter was temporary and served a purpose. It had prompted the Corinthians to reflect on their actions and spiritual condition, leading to repentance and positive change.

This verse reflects the delicate balance that Paul had to maintain in his correspondence with the Corinthians. While he initially regretted causing them sorrow, he ultimately saw the benefit of addressing their issues.

Verse 9 (2 Corinthians 7:9, KJV):

"Now I rejoice, not that ye were made sorry, but that ye sorrowed to repentance: for ye were made sorry after a godly manner, that ye might receive damage by us in nothing."

Expository Commentary on Verse 9:

In this verse, Paul clarifies his perspective on the Corinthians' sorrow and the positive outcome it had achieved.

- "Now I rejoice, not that ye were made sorry," - Paul makes it clear that his joy does not stem from the fact that he caused them sorrow through his letter. He did not take pleasure in their distress.

- "but that ye sorrowed to repentance:" - His joy arises from the fact that their sorrow led to genuine repentance. The Corinthians' response to the sorrow was a turning point in their behavior and attitudes.

- "for ye were made sorry after a godly manner," - Paul underscores the quality of their sorrow. It was not mere worldly sorrow but sorrow that reflected a godly attitude and response. Their sorrow led to spiritual change and growth.

- "that ye might receive damage by us in nothing." - The Corinthians' godly sorrow ensured that they suffered no spiritual harm or damage from Paul's corrective words. Instead, it resulted in positive spiritual growth.

This verse highlights the distinction between mere worldly sorrow and godly sorrow that leads to repentance and positive transformation. Paul commends the Corinthians for their godly response.

Verse 10 (2 Corinthians 7:10, KJV):

"For godly sorrow worketh repentance to salvation not to be repented of: but the sorrow of the world worketh death."

Expository Commentary on Verse 10:

In this verse, Paul further explains the distinction between godly sorrow and worldly sorrow.

- "For godly sorrow worketh repentance to salvation not to be repented of:" - Paul emphasizes the positive and transformative nature of godly sorrow. When individuals experience sorrow in response to their sins or wrongdoings and it leads to genuine repentance, it results in salvation and a transformation of their lives. This is a permanent change that does not need to be regretted.

- "but the sorrow of the world worketh death." - In contrast, worldly sorrow, which is characterized by regret, guilt, and despair without true repentance, leads to spiritual death and separation from God.

This verse underscores the vital distinction between two types of sorrow: godly sorrow that leads to salvation and transformation and worldly sorrow that leads to spiritual death.

Verse 11 (2 Corinthians 7:11, KJV):

"For behold this selfsame thing, that ye sorrowed after a godly sort, what carefulness it wrought in you, yea, what clearing of yourselves, yea, what indignation, yea, what fear, yea, what vehement desire, yea, what zeal, yea, what revenge! In all things ye have approved yourselves to be clear in this matter."

Expository Commentary on Verse 11:

In this verse, Paul lists the positive outcomes of the Corinthians' godly sorrow and genuine repentance.

- "For behold this selfsame thing," - Paul draws attention to the fact that the Corinthians experienced godly sorrow and the resulting transformation. He then proceeds to describe the tangible results of this process.

- "that ye sorrowed after a godly sort," - The Corinthians' sorrow was indeed godly in nature, leading to the following outcomes.

- "what carefulness it wrought in you," - Their godly sorrow produced a sense of earnest care and diligence in their spiritual lives. They became more conscientious and watchful.

- "yea, what clearing of yourselves," - They actively worked to clear themselves of the sins and issues that had caused their sorrow. They took responsibility and made amends.

- "yea, what indignation," - The Corinthians felt righteous anger and indignation toward the sins they had committed, recognizing them as offensive to God.

- "yea, what fear," - Their godly sorrow led to a reverential fear of God and a desire to avoid further wrongdoing.

- "yea, what vehement desire," - They developed a passionate desire for righteousness and holiness.

- "yea, what zeal," - Their godly sorrow ignited a fervent zeal for God's ways and purposes.

- "yea, what revenge!" - They sought to right the wrongs and injustices they had committed or allowed.

- "In all things ye have approved yourselves to be clear in this matter." - In summary, the Corinthians demonstrated their sincerity and genuine repentance by their actions and attitudes. They proved themselves to be blameless in the matter that had caused their initial sorrow.

This verse illustrates the powerful impact of godly sorrow when it leads to true repentance. It results in a profound transformation and a strong desire for righteousness and holiness.

Verse 12 (2 Corinthians 7:12, KJV):

"Wherefore, though I wrote unto you, I did it not for his cause that had done the wrong, nor for his cause that suffered wrong, but that our care for you in the sight of God might appear unto you."

Expository Commentary on Verse 12:

Paul provides the underlying motivation for his previous letter and actions regarding the Corinthians' situation.

- "Wherefore, though I wrote unto you," - Paul refers to the letter he had previously written to the Corinthians, which addressed the issues within the church.

- "I did it not for his cause that had done the wrong," - Paul clarifies that his primary motive for writing the letter was not solely

to address the wrongdoer or the one who had been wronged. It was not about assigning blame or justice in that specific case.

- "nor for his cause that suffered wrong," - Paul reiterates that his primary concern was not to vindicate the one who had suffered the wrongdoing.

- "but that our care for you in the sight of God might appear unto you." - The central reason for Paul's actions and the letter was to demonstrate his deep care and concern for the Corinthians in the presence of God. He wanted them to understand the depth of his love and commitment to their spiritual well-being.

This verse reveals Paul's overarching concern for the Corinthians' spiritual growth and his desire for them to perceive his genuine care for their welfare.

Verse 13 (2 Corinthians 7:13, KJV):

"Therefore we were comforted in your comfort: yea, and exceedingly the more joyed we for the joy of Titus, because his spirit was refreshed by you all."

Expository Commentary on Verse 13:

In this verse, Paul shares how the Corinthians' comfort brought comfort and joy to him and Titus.

- "Therefore we were comforted in your comfort:" - Paul and his companions found comfort and solace in the fact that the Corinthians had received comfort through their godly sorrow and repentance.

- "yea, and exceedingly the more joyed we for the joy of Titus," - The Corinthians' positive response, which had brought joy to Titus, also brought increased joy to Paul and his team. Titus's joy and positive experience among the Corinthians were a source of great happiness for them.

- "because his spirit was refreshed by you all." - Titus's spirits were uplifted and refreshed by the Corinthians. Their repentance and transformation had a positive impact on him.

This verse underscores the interrelatedness of emotions and experiences within the Christian community. The Corinthians' repentance brought joy to Paul, Titus, and the entire Christian fellowship. It exemplifies the mutual encouragement and support that believers can provide one another in their faith journey.

Verse 14 (2 Corinthians 7:14, KJV):

"For if I have boasted anything to him of you, I am not ashamed; but as we spake all things to you in truth, even so our boasting, which I made before Titus, is found a truth."

Expository Commentary on Verse 14:

In this verse, Paul speaks about his earlier boasts to Titus concerning the Corinthians.

- "For if I have boasted anything to him of you," - Paul had previously made positive statements or boasts about the Corinthians to Titus. He had likely commended their response to his previous letter and their repentance.

- "I am not ashamed;" - Paul does not regret or feel embarrassed about the positive things he had said about the Corinthians to Titus. He is confident in the Corinthians' actions and character.

- "but as we spoke all things to you in truth," - Paul reminds the Corinthians that all his previous words to them were spoken in truth and sincerity. His boasting about them was not based on falsehood.

- "even so our boasting, which I made before Titus, is found a truth." - Paul affirms that the Corinthians' actions and repentance have validated his earlier boasts about them to Titus. The positive things he said about them have been proven true.

This verse underscores the integrity of Paul's communication and his confidence in the Corinthians' response to his previous letter.

Verse 15 (2 Corinthians 7:15, KJV):

"And his inward affection is more abundant toward you, whilst he remembereth the obedience of you all, how with fear and trembling ye received him."

Expository Commentary on Verse 15:

In this verse, Paul describes Titus's increased affection for the Corinthians and their obedient response to him.

- "And his inward affection is more abundant toward you," - Titus's love and affection for the Corinthians have grown even stronger. His heart is filled with deep love for them.

- "whilst he remembereth the obedience of you all," - Titus's affection intensifies as he recalls the Corinthians' obedience. They had responded obediently to his message and the instructions he conveyed from Paul.

- "how with fear and trembling ye received him." - The Corinthians' obedience was marked by a sense of reverence and humility. They received Titus with a deep sense of awe and respect, recognizing the importance of the message he brought.

This verse highlights the positive response of the Corinthians to Titus and the impact of their obedience on his affection for them.

Verse 16 (2 Corinthians 7:16, KJV):

"I rejoice therefore that I have confidence in you in all things."

Expository Commentary on Verse 16:

In this verse, Paul expresses his joy and confidence in the Corinthians.

- "I rejoice therefore," - Paul's feelings of joy are linked to what he has observed and the confidence he has in the Corinthians.

- "that I have confidence in you in all things." - Paul's joy stems from his confidence in the Corinthians in all matters. He is reassured by their positive response and obedience to Titus and is confident in their willingness to follow his guidance and instructions.

This verse signifies Paul's deep satisfaction and trust in the Corinthians, particularly in their response to his previous letter and their obedience to Titus. It reflects his anticipation of continued growth and cooperation with them in the future.

Chapter 8
The Grace of Giving

The theme of 2 Corinthians Chapter 8 is the grace of giving and the willingness of the Corinthian church to participate in a collection for the saints in Jerusalem. In this chapter, the apostle Paul commends the Corinthian believers for their generosity and encourages them to complete their financial contribution.

Key themes in 2 Corinthians Chapter 8 include:

1. Grace of Giving: The central theme is the grace of giving, emphasizing the Corinthians' willingness to contribute to the financial support of the saints in Jerusalem. Paul highlights the act of giving as an expression of God's grace.

2. Generosity and Willingness: Paul commends the Corinthians for their generosity and willingness to participate in the collection. He uses the Macedonian churches as an example of cheerful giving and encourages the Corinthians to excel in this grace of giving.

3. Equality and Fairness: Paul speaks about equality and fairness in giving, noting that their abundance should supply the lack of others. He encourages a sense of equity in the distribution of resources among believers.

4. Example of Christ's Giving: Paul cites the example of Jesus Christ, who, though rich, became poor for the sake of humanity. He encourages the Corinthians to follow Christ's example in their giving.

5. Completion of the Collection: The chapter discusses the need to complete the collection and emphasizes the importance of integrity and accountability in handling financial matters.

In summary, 2 Corinthians Chapter 8 centers around the theme of the grace of giving, highlighting the Corinthians' willingness to participate in the collection for the saints in Jerusalem. It underscores the principles of generosity, equality, and following the example of Christ in the context of financial support for fellow believers in need.

Verse 1 (2 Corinthians 8:1, KJV):

"Moreover, brethren, we do you to wit of the grace of God bestowed on the churches of Macedonia;"

Expository Commentary on Verse 1:

In this verse, Paul begins to address the Corinthians regarding the generosity of the Macedonian churches.

- "Moreover, brethren," - Paul addresses the Corinthians as brethren, emphasizing their shared identity as fellow believers.

- "we do you to wit of the grace of God bestowed on the churches of Macedonia;" - Paul informs the Corinthians about the grace of God that had been generously poured out upon the churches in Macedonia. This grace is associated with their acts of kindness and generosity, which Paul is about to describe.

Verse 2 (2 Corinthians 8:2, KJV):

"How that in a great trial of affliction the abundance of their joy and their deep poverty abounded unto the riches of their liberality."

Expository Commentary on Verse 2:

Paul highlights the remarkable response of the Macedonian churches to their challenging circumstances.

- "How that in a great trial of affliction," - The Macedonian churches were enduring a severe test of their faith and endurance, likely facing various trials and difficulties.

- "the abundance of their joy" - Despite the adversity, the Macedonian believers experienced an overflowing joy. Their joy was not diminished by their hardships.

- "and their deep poverty" - At the same time, they were in a state of profound poverty. Their resources were limited, and they faced economic challenges.

- "abounded unto the riches of their liberality." - Remarkably, their joy and spiritual wealth overflowed into a rich display of liberality and generosity. Despite their poverty, they gave generously and willingly.

This verse illustrates the paradox of the Macedonian churches' situation: their great joy in the midst of suffering and their generous giving despite their poverty. It serves as an example of sacrificial giving and joyful generosity.

Verse 3 (2 Corinthians 8:3, KJV):

"For to their power, I bear record, yea, and beyond their power they were willing of themselves;"

Expository Commentary on Verse 3:

Paul continues to describe the extraordinary willingness of the Macedonian believers to contribute to the needs of others.

- "For to their power, I bear record," - Paul testifies that the Macedonians gave to the extent of their ability. They gave according to their means, as he can attest.

- "yea, and beyond their power they were willing of themselves;" - What is truly remarkable is that the Macedonians went above and beyond their own capacity to give. They did this voluntarily and with eagerness.

This verse emphasizes not only the extent of their giving but also the eager and self-motivated nature of their generosity.

Verse 4 (2 Corinthians 8:4, KJV):

"Praying us with much intreaty that we would receive the gift and take upon us the fellowship of the ministering to the saints."

Expository Commentary on Verse 4:

Paul describes how the Macedonian believers earnestly requested that he and his companions accept their gift and participate in ministering to the needs of the saints.

- "Praying us with much intreaty" - The Macedonian Christians implored Paul and his team with strong, earnest requests. They were determined to contribute to the needs of the saints.

- "that we would receive the gift," - They asked Paul to accept the gift they had prepared for the benefit of the saints.

- "and take upon us the fellowship of the ministering to the saints." - The Macedonians wanted Paul to actively participate in the ministry of providing for the needs of fellow believers. They sought to be partners with Paul in this service.

This verse illustrates the eager desire of the Macedonian believers to share in the ministry of helping fellow Christians in need and their insistence that Paul and his companions accept their contribution.

Verse 5 (2 Corinthians 8:5, KJV):

"And this they did, not as we hoped, but first gave their own selves to the Lord, and unto us by the will of God."

Expository Commentary on Verse 5:

Paul further explains the Macedonians' approach to giving.

- "And this they did, not as we hoped," - The Macedonians' generosity exceeded Paul's expectations. They did more than he had anticipated.

- "but first gave their own selves to the Lord," - The primary and foundational act of the Macedonians was to dedicate themselves to the Lord. They offered their own lives in devotion to God, surrendering themselves completely.

- "and unto us by the will of God." - In addition to their commitment to God, they also recognized the role of Paul and his team in God's plan. They willingly submitted to the apostolic authority, acknowledging that it was God's will for them to do so.

This verse underscores the Macedonian believers' deep commitment to God and their recognition of the divine will in their relationship with Paul and his ministry.

Verse 6 (2 Corinthians 8:6, KJV):

"Insomuch that we desired Titus, that as he had begun, so he would also finish in you the same grace also."

Expository Commentary on Verse 6:

Paul expresses his desire for Titus to complete the work of collecting the Corinthians' offering as he had done among the Macedonian churches.

- "Insomuch that we desired Titus," - Paul and his team had a strong desire and plan for Titus regarding the collection of the Corinthians' offering.

- "that as he had begun," - Titus had initiated the process of collecting the offering, likely among the Macedonians.

- "so he would also finish in you the same grace also." - Paul wanted Titus to complete the work he had started among the Corinthians, with the same grace and generosity displayed by the Macedonian churches.

This verse highlights the continuity and consistency of the collection process among the churches, emphasizing the unity in giving and sharing of God's grace.

Verse 7 (2 Corinthians 8:7, KJV):

"Therefore, as ye abound in everything, in faith, and utterance, and knowledge, and in all diligence, and in your love to us, see that ye abound in this grace also."

Expository Commentary on Verse 7:

In this verse, Paul encourages the Corinthians to excel in the grace of giving, just as they excel in other areas of their Christian walk.

- "Therefore, as ye abound in everything," - Paul acknowledges that the Corinthians excel in various aspects of their faith and Christian life. They have abundant faith, the ability to express themselves effectively, knowledge, diligence, and love for the apostles.

- "in faith, and utterance, and knowledge, and in all diligence, and in your love to us," - These are areas in which the Corinthians excel. They have a strong faith, are effective in expressing themselves, possess knowledge, work diligently, and love the apostles.

- "see that ye abound in this grace also." - Paul urges the Corinthians to also excel in the area of grace, particularly in the context of giving. He wants them to be generous and share in the act of giving to support the needs of others.

This verse encourages the Corinthians to extend their excellence in faith and other virtues to the practice of generous giving, emphasizing the importance of sharing in this grace. It underscores the holistic nature of Christian living, which includes both faith and acts of love and charity.

Verse 8 (2 Corinthians 8:8, KJV):

"I speak not by commandment, but by occasion of the forwardness of others, and to prove the sincerity of your love."

Expository Commentary on Verse 8:

In this verse, Paul explains his approach to the Corinthians regarding giving and support for the saints.

- "I speak not by commandment," - Paul clarifies that he is not giving a command or imposing an obligation upon the Corinthians. He is not issuing a directive that they must follow.

- "but by occasion of the forwardness of others," - Instead, his encouragement for giving is prompted by the eagerness and willingness demonstrated by others. The example of the Macedonian churches, who gave generously, has inspired him to address the Corinthians on this matter.

- "and to prove the sincerity of your love." - Paul's primary purpose in addressing the Corinthians about giving is to test and demonstrate the genuineness of their love. He wants to see if their love for the saints and their commitment to God's work are sincere.

This verse underscores that Paul is not forcing the Corinthians to give but is encouraging them based on the example of others and the opportunity to demonstrate their love through generous giving.

Verse 9 (2 Corinthians 8:9, KJV):

"For ye know the grace of our Lord Jesus Christ, that, though he was rich, yet for your sakes he became poor, that ye through his poverty might be rich."

Expository Commentary on Verse 9:

In this verse, Paul invokes the example of Jesus Christ as the ultimate motivation for generosity.

- "For ye know the grace of our Lord Jesus Christ," - Paul reminds the Corinthians of their knowledge of the grace (unmerited favor) demonstrated by Jesus Christ. He is pointing to the generosity of Christ as an example.

- "that, though he was rich," - Before His incarnation, Jesus existed in the richness of His divine glory. He shared in the eternal wealth of the Godhead.

- "yet for your sakes he became poor," - Despite His divine richness, Jesus willingly took on the form of a poor and humble human being. He became incarnate for the sake of humanity, experiencing poverty and the limitations of human existence.

- "that ye through his poverty might be rich." - The purpose of Jesus' voluntary poverty was to bring spiritual riches to humanity. Through His sacrificial death on the cross, He offers the wealth of salvation, forgiveness, and eternal life to all who believe in Him.

This verse is a powerful reminder of the sacrificial love and generosity of Jesus Christ. It encourages believers to imitate Christ's selflessness by sharing their material blessings with others, especially those in need. It also underscores the spiritual wealth that comes through Christ's redemptive work.

Verse 10 (2 Corinthians 8:10, KJV):

"And herein I give my advice: for this is expedient for you, who have begun before, not only to do, but also to be forward a year ago."

Expository Commentary on Verse 10:

In this verse, Paul offers his counsel and emphasizes the importance of completing the giving project that the Corinthians had started.

- "And herein I give my advice:" - Paul presents his counsel to the Corinthians regarding their participation in the collection for the saints in Jerusalem. He is offering guidance.

- "for this is expedient for you," - Paul explains that what he is advising is beneficial and advantageous for the Corinthians. It will work to their advantage.

- "who have begun before," - The Corinthians had already initiated the process of collecting funds for the saints in Jerusalem. They had taken the first step.

- "not only to do, but also to be forward a year ago." - Paul commends the Corinthians for their initial willingness to give, but he also notes that their eagerness and readiness to give had been evident a year earlier. He encourages them to continue and complete what they had started.

This verse underscores the need for the Corinthians to follow through with their commitment to giving and to complete what they had begun a year ago. Paul's advice is based on the principle of fulfilling their good intentions.

Verse 11 (2 Corinthians 8:11, KJV):
"Now therefore perform the doing of it; that as there was a readiness to will, so there may be a performance also out of that which ye have."

Expository Commentary on Verse 11:

Paul urges the Corinthians to take action and carry out their good intentions regarding giving.

- "Now therefore perform the doing of it;" - Paul calls upon the Corinthians to act on their desire to give. He encourages them to put their intentions into action.

- "that as there was a readiness to will," - The Corinthians had previously shown an eagerness and willingness to give. They had the right intentions.

- "so there may be a performance also out of that which ye have." - Paul wants the Corinthians to translate their good intentions into tangible actions, using the resources they possess to complete the act of giving.

This verse emphasizes the need for the Corinthians to follow through on their willingness to give by taking concrete steps to fulfill their commitment.

Verse 12 (2 Corinthians 8:12, KJV):

"For if there be first a willing mind, it is accepted according to that a man hath, and not according to that he hath not."

Expository Commentary on Verse 12:

Paul explains the principle of giving in a way that considers one's willingness and available resources.

- "For if there be first a willing mind," - The key to giving is a willing and generous attitude. The starting point is the desire to give and help others.

- "it is accepted according to that a man hath," - Paul makes it clear that God accepts a person's offering based on what they have, not on what they do not have. It is a matter of the heart and the willingness to give, not the amount.

- "and not according to that he hath not." - God does not require individuals to give beyond their means or resources. The emphasis is on giving joyfully and sacrificially based on what one can give.

This verse underscores the principle of proportional giving, where the willingness of the heart is more important than the amount given. It also promotes fairness and takes into account people's varying financial situations and abilities to give.

Verse 13 (2 Corinthians 8:13, KJV):

"For I mean not that other men be eased, and ye burdened:"

Expository Commentary on Verse 13:

In this verse, Paul clarifies his intention regarding giving, emphasizing that his goal is not to shift the burden from one group to another.

- "For I mean not that other men be eased," - Paul begins by explaining that his purpose is not to make the burden of giving lighter for one group of believers at the expense of another.

- "and ye burdened:" - He also does not intend to place a heavy financial burden on the Corinthians.

This verse highlights Paul's concern for fairness and equity in matters of giving. He doesn't want the Corinthians to bear an excessive financial burden, nor does he want other believers to be completely relieved of their responsibility. Instead, he seeks a balanced approach to sharing resources.

Verse 14 (2 Corinthians 8:14, KJV):

"But by an equality, that now at this time your abundance may be a supply for their want, that their abundance also may be a supply for your want: that there may be equality:"

Expository Commentary on Verse 14:

In this verse, Paul explains his concept of equality in giving and sharing resources.

- "But by an equality," - Paul's goal is to establish a sense of fairness and balance in the distribution of resources.

- "that now at this time your abundance may be a supply for their want," - He envisions a situation where the Corinthians, who have an abundance, can provide for the needs of those who are lacking or in want.

- "that their abundance also may be a supply for your want:" - Likewise, when the circumstances are reversed, and the Corinthians are in need, he hopes that those who were once in need will be able to provide for them.

- "that there may be equality:" - The ultimate aim is to achieve equality, where there is a fair and balanced sharing of resources among believers.

This verse emphasizes the principle of mutual support and shared responsibility among believers. It encourages the Corinthians to provide for the needs of others when they have the means and to receive help from others when they are in need, creating a sense of equality within the community of faith.

Verse 15 (2 Corinthians 8:15, KJV):

"As it is written, He that had gathered much had nothing over, and he that had gathered little had no lack."

Expository Commentary on Verse 15:

In this verse, Paul quotes from the Old Testament to support his principle of equality in giving.

- "As it is written," - Paul references a scriptural passage to validate his point.

- "He that had gathered much had nothing over," - This phrase is a reference to the gathering of manna in the wilderness during the time of Moses. Those who gathered a lot of manna did not have any surplus, and it was meant to be shared and eaten the same day.

- "and he that had gathered little had no lack." - Similarly, those who gathered less manna did not go hungry because they had enough for their needs.

Paul uses this Old Testament example to illustrate the principle of sharing and equality. In the same way, believers should be willing to share their abundance with those in need, so that everyone has enough.

This verse emphasizes the idea that the principle of equality in giving is not a new concept but has its roots in the Old Testament. It underscores the importance of sharing and providing for one another's needs within the Christian community.

Verse 16 (2 Corinthians 8:16, KJV):

"But thanks be to God, which put the same earnest care into the heart of Titus for you."

Expository Commentary on Verse 16:

In this verse, Paul expresses gratitude to God for instilling a deep concern for the Corinthians in Titus.

- "But thanks be to God," - Paul begins by acknowledging God's role in the situation, recognizing that it is God who has worked to produce this caring disposition in Titus.

- "which put the same earnest care into the heart of Titus for you." - Paul credits God for instilling in Titus the same fervent care and concern for the Corinthians that he himself has. Titus shares Paul's deep affection for the Corinthians and is motivated by the same sense of responsibility.

This verse emphasizes God's providential work in raising up individuals like Titus who genuinely care for the welfare and well-being of others within the Christian community.

Verse 17 (2 Corinthians 8:17, KJV):

"For indeed he accepted the exhortation; but being more forward, of his own accord he went unto you."

Expository Commentary on Verse 17:

Paul explains Titus's response to his exhortation and willingness to visit the Corinthians.

- "For indeed he accepted the exhortation;" - Titus heeded Paul's counsel and accepted the encouragement to visit the Corinthians.

- "but being more forward, of his own accord he went unto you." - In addition to accepting the exhortation, Titus showed a strong eagerness and initiative by deciding on his own to go to the Corinthians. He went willingly and voluntarily.

This verse underscores Titus's willingness and eagerness to fulfill the mission to the Corinthians, even going beyond what was initially exhorted. His actions exemplify his deep concern for their welfare.

Verse 18 (2 Corinthians 8:18, KJV):

"And we have sent with him the brother, whose praise is in the gospel throughout all the churches;"

Expository Commentary on Verse 18:

In this verse, Paul mentions that he has sent a highly regarded brother along with Titus.

- "And we have sent with him the brother," - Paul, along with others, has chosen to send a fellow believer in the company of Titus.

- "whose praise is in the gospel throughout all the churches;" - This brother is highly esteemed and has earned a good reputation among the churches for his service and ministry in the spreading of the gospel. He is known for his dedication to the work of the gospel.

This verse introduces the presence of a respected and trustworthy individual who will accompany Titus on the mission to the Corinthians. His reputation in the churches is a testament to his commitment to the gospel.

Verse 19 (2 Corinthians 8:19, KJV):

"And not that only, but who was also chosen of the churches to travel with us with this grace, which is administered by us to the glory of the same Lord, and declaration of your ready mind:"

Expository Commentary on Verse 19:

Paul provides additional information about the chosen brother and his role in the mission.

- "And not that only, but who was also chosen of the churches to travel with us with this grace," - This brother was not only highly praised but was also selected by the churches to accompany Paul and his team on this mission. He was chosen to participate in the administration of the grace that the churches provided.

- "which is administered by us to the glory of the same Lord," - The grace they are administering, which includes the financial contributions from the churches, is done for the glory of the Lord. It is a service that brings honor and praise to the Lord.

- "and declaration of your ready mind:" - Additionally, this mission serves to publicly express the Corinthians' willing and eager attitude toward supporting the needs of others. It is a testimony to their readiness to help.

This verse underscores the cooperative nature of the mission, where the chosen brother is working alongside Paul and his team to administer the grace provided by the churches, all for the glory of the Lord and as an expression of the Corinthians' eagerness to help.

Verse 20 (2 Corinthians 8:20, KJV):

"Avoiding this, that no man should blame us in this abundance which is administered by us:"

Expository Commentary on Verse 20:

In this verse, Paul explains his precautionary approach in handling financial contributions.

- "Avoiding this," - Paul and his companions are taking care to prevent a particular situation.

- "that no man should blame us in this abundance which is administered by us:" - They want to ensure that no one can criticize or find fault with the way they handle the substantial number of resources entrusted to them for administration.

This verse reveals Paul's commitment to transparency and accountability in financial matters, as he seeks to protect his integrity and that of his ministry.

Verse 21 (2 Corinthians 8:21, KJV):

"Providing for honest things, not only in the sight of the Lord, but also in the sight of men."

Expository Commentary on Verse 21:

Paul explains his approach to handling financial matters, emphasizing both godly and human accountability.

- "Providing for honest things," - Paul and his team are ensuring that everything they do in administering the finances is marked by integrity and uprightness. They take measures to guarantee that their actions are honorable.

- "not only in the sight of the Lord," - Their primary accountability is to the Lord. They are conscious of His oversight and judgment in their financial stewardship.

- "but also in the sight of men." - In addition to their accountability to God, they are also mindful of how their actions appear to other people. They strive to maintain a good reputation and avoid any accusations of mishandling funds.

This verse highlights the importance of both spiritual and practical integrity in financial matters, with a commitment to do what is right in the eyes of both God and people. It reflects Paul's desire to maintain a blameless testimony in financial stewardship.

Verse 22 (2 Corinthians 8:22, KJV):

"And we have sent with them our brother, whom we have oftentimes proved diligent in many things, but now much more diligent, upon the great confidence which I have in you."

Expository Commentary on Verse 22:

In this verse, Paul introduces another brother who is being sent along with others for the mission to the Corinthians.

- "And we have sent with them our brother," - Paul mentions that they have included another fellow believer in the group sent to the Corinthians.

- "whom we have oftentimes proved diligent in many things," - This brother has been tested and proven to be hardworking and diligent on numerous occasions in various matters or circumstances.

- "but now much more diligent," - Paul highlights that this brother's diligence has grown even more, likely in response to the situation at hand.

- "upon the great confidence which I have in you." - Paul's confidence in the Corinthians has influenced the selection of this diligent brother to be part of the mission. He trusts that their willingness to support the work will be a motivating factor for this brother's increased diligence.

This verse emphasizes the selection of individuals with a track record of diligence and their increased commitment to the mission based on the Corinthians' responsiveness.

Verse 23 (2 Corinthians 8:23, KJV):

"Whether any do enquire of Titus, he is my partner and fellow helper concerning you: or our brethren be enquired of, they are the messengers of the churches, and the glory of Christ."

Expository Commentary on Verse 23:

Paul provides additional information about the roles of Titus and the other brethren in the mission.

- "Whether any do enquire of Titus, he is my partner and fellow helper concerning you:" - Paul makes it clear that Titus is closely associated with him, serving as a partner and co-laborer in the ministry to the Corinthians. He is well-informed about the Corinthians and their needs.

- "or our brethren be enquired of," - If anyone has questions about the other brethren accompanying Titus, Paul wants to assure the Corinthians that they are also reliable and well-equipped for the mission.

- "they are the messengers of the churches," - These brethren serve as representatives and messengers of the various churches that have contributed to the mission. They carry the collective support and offerings of these churches.

- "and the glory of Christ." - These brethren's service in the mission reflects the glory of Christ. Their actions bring honor and praise to the Lord.

This verse emphasizes the qualifications and roles of Titus and the other brethren in the mission, highlighting their close association with Paul and their representation of the contributing churches, all for the glory of Christ.

Verse 24 (2 Corinthians 8:24, KJV):

"Wherefore shew ye to them, and before the churches, the proof of your love, and of our boasting on your behalf."

Expository Commentary on Verse 24:

In this final verse of the chapter, Paul encourages the Corinthians to demonstrate their love and the validity of Paul's boasting on their behalf.

- "Wherefore shew ye to them," - Paul urges the Corinthians to reveal, display, or manifest something.

- "and before the churches," - The Corinthians are encouraged to do this not only in the presence of those accompanying Titus but also in the presence of representatives from other churches.

- "the proof of your love," - The Corinthians are to provide evidence or a demonstration of their genuine love, particularly in the context of supporting the mission and those in need.

- "and of our boasting on your behalf." - This is an opportunity for the Corinthians to prove that Paul's positive comments and boasting about their willingness to give and support the work were well-founded and accurate.

This verse underscores the importance of the Corinthians' actions serving as a testament to their love and the validity of Paul's commendation of their generosity and support. It emphasizes the need for consistency between words and deeds in demonstrating their love for others.

Chapter 9
Generosity in Giving and the Blessing that results from a Cheerful and Purposeful act of Giving

The theme of 2 Corinthians Chapter 9 is generosity in giving and the blessings that result from a cheerful and purposeful act of giving. In this chapter, the apostle Paul continues to address the collection for the saints in Jerusalem and emphasizes the principles of sowing and reaping in the context of giving.

Key themes in 2 Corinthians Chapter 9 include:

1. Generosity and Cheerful Giving: The central theme is the call for believers to give generously and cheerfully. Paul encourages the Corinthians to be willing and generous contributors to the collection for the saints.

2. Blessings of Giving: Paul emphasizes that those who sow sparingly will reap sparingly, while those who sow bountifully will reap bountifully. He underscores the idea that God loves a cheerful giver and that giving is a source of blessings.

3. Provision and Abundance: The chapter speaks of God's ability to provide for the Corinthians in abundance. Paul believes that their generosity will result in an abundant provision of their needs.

4. Thanksgiving and Gratitude: Paul expresses his gratitude for the Corinthians' willingness to participate in the collection, highlighting their track record of support and partnership in ministry.

5. Fulfillment of Promises: Paul assures the Corinthians that he will send representatives to ensure that the collection is prepared as promised. He wants to avoid any embarrassment and desires the Corinthians to have their gift ready as a willing, cheerful contribution.

In summary, 2 Corinthians Chapter 9 revolves around the theme of generosity in giving, emphasizing the blessings that come from a cheerful and purposeful act of giving. It encourages believers to be generous and willing contributors, underlining the principles of sowing and reaping in the context of financial support for those in need.

Verse 1 (2 Corinthians 9:1, KJV):

"For as touching the ministering to the saints, it is superfluous for me to write to you:"

Expository Commentary on Verse 1:

In this verse, Paul begins by addressing the Corinthians regarding their ministry to the saints in Jerusalem.

- "For as touching the ministering to the saints," - Paul is referring to the collection of offerings and support that the Corinthians are providing for the saints in Jerusalem, who are in need.

- "it is superfluous for me to write to you:" - Paul suggests that there is no need for him to write extensively or repeatedly on this matter. The Corinthians are already aware of their responsibility in this regard.

This verse highlights the Corinthians' existing knowledge and understanding of the ministry to the saints, and it indicates that Paul does not need to provide extensive instructions on the subject.

Verse 2 (2 Corinthians 9:2, KJV):

"For I know the forwardness of your mind, for which I boast of you to them of Macedonia, that Achaia was ready a year ago, and your zeal hath provoked very many."

Expository Commentary on Verse 2:

In this verse, Paul acknowledges the Corinthians' eagerness and willingness to participate in the collection for the saints.

- "For I know the forwardness of your mind," - Paul is aware of the eagerness and readiness of the Corinthians to contribute and help.

- "for which I boast of you to them of Macedonia," - Paul takes pride in telling the Macedonian believers about the Corinthians' enthusiastic response to the call for support. He uses the Corinthians' example to inspire and encourage other regions to also contribute.

- "that Achaia was ready a year ago," - Paul commends the readiness of Achaia, the broader region that includes Corinth, which had been prepared to contribute a year ago.

- "and your zeal hath provoked very many." - The Corinthians' fervor and enthusiasm have stirred many others to take action and get involved in supporting the saints in need.

This verse emphasizes the Corinthians' zeal and their positive influence on others in the region. Their eagerness to give has served as a source of motivation and encouragement for believers in other areas.

Verse 3 (2 Corinthians 9:3, KKV):

"Yet have I sent the brethren, lest our boasting of you should be in vain in this behalf; that, as I said, ye may be ready:"

Expository Commentary on Verse 3:

In this verse, Paul explains his decision to send brethren to the Corinthians despite their readiness.

- "Yet have I sent the brethren," - Paul has still chosen to send a group of fellow believers to Corinth.

- "lest our boasting of you should be in vain in this behalf;" - Paul is concerned that his previous boasting about the Corinthians' preparedness and willingness to give would be proven empty or groundless if the Corinthians were not actually ready to fulfill their commitment.

- "that, as I said, ye may be ready:" - Paul's intention in sending the brethren is to ensure that the Corinthians are indeed prepared to participate in the collection and fulfill their commitment, as he had previously mentioned.

This verse reveals Paul's desire for the Corinthians' actions to align with their reputation, so he sends the brethren to confirm their readiness.

Verse 4 (2 Corinthians 9:4, KJV):

"Lest haply if they of Macedonia come with me, and find you unprepared, we (that we say not, ye) should be ashamed in this same confident boasting."

Expository Commentary on Verse 4:

In this verse, Paul expresses his concern about the Corinthians' readiness to give when he arrives with the Macedonian believers.

- "Lest haply if they of Macedonia come with me, and find you unprepared," - Paul is concerned that if he, along with the Macedonian believers, were to arrive in Corinth and find the Corinthians unprepared to contribute, it would be embarrassing.

- "we (that we say not, ye) should be ashamed in this same confident boasting." - Paul clarifies that it is not the Corinthians themselves but he and the Macedonians who would feel ashamed for having confidently boasted about the Corinthians' readiness to give. It is a matter of maintaining their reputation.

This verse emphasizes the need for the Corinthians to be prepared to fulfill their commitment, as not doing so would lead to embarrassment and disappointment for Paul and the Macedonians.

Verse 5 (2 Corinthians 9:5, KJV):

"Therefore, I thought it necessary to exhort the brethren, that they would go before unto you, and make up beforehand your bounty, whereof ye had notice before, that the same might be ready, as a matter of bounty, and not as of covetousness."

Expository Commentary on Verse 5:

In this verse, Paul explains his decision to send brethren ahead to ensure the Corinthians are ready for their contribution.

- "Therefore, I thought it necessary to exhort the brethren," - Paul considered it important and necessary to encourage the brethren to go to the Corinthians.

- "that they would go before unto you, and make up beforehand your bounty," - He wanted the brethren to go in advance to Corinth and help the Corinthians prepare their generous contribution.

- "whereof ye had notice before," - The Corinthians had been informed in advance about this collection and their participation in it.

- "that the same might be ready, as a matter of bounty, and not as of covetousness." - Paul's goal is to ensure that the Corinthians' contribution is ready, willingly given, and motivated by a generous spirit rather than any sense of greed or covetousness.

This verse underscores Paul's careful planning and consideration of the Corinthians' readiness and the proper motivation behind their giving. He wants their contribution to be a genuine act of generosity and not driven by self-interest.

Verse 6 (2 Corinthians 9:6, KJV):

"But this I say, He which soweth sparingly shall reap also sparingly, and he which soweth bountifully shall reap also bountifully."

Expository Commentary on Verse 6:

In this verse, Paul employs an agricultural analogy to convey a principle of generosity and reaping.

- "But this I say," - Paul introduces an important principle he wants to emphasize.

- "He which soweth sparingly shall reap also sparingly," - Just as a farmer who sows only a few seeds will have a limited harvest, so, too, a person who gives sparingly will receive only a modest return.

- "and he which soweth bountifully shall reap also bountifully." - Conversely, the one who sows generously and abundantly will reap a correspondingly generous and abundant harvest.

This verse emphasizes the spiritual principle of sowing and reaping in the context of giving. It encourages believers to give generously, knowing that their generosity will be rewarded in kindness.

Verse 7 (2 Corinthians 9:7, KJV):

"Every man according as he purposeth in his heart, so let him give; not grudgingly, or of necessity: for God loveth a cheerful giver."

Expository Commentary on Verse 7:

In this verse, Paul provides guidance on the attitude and manner of giving.

- "Every man according as he purposeth in his heart, so let him give;" - Paul instructs that each person should give as they have determined in their own heart. Giving should be a matter of personal conviction and purpose.

- "not grudgingly, or of necessity:" - Giving should not be done reluctantly or out of a sense of obligation or compulsion.

- "for God loveth a cheerful giver." - God delights in and has a special affection for those who give with a cheerful and willing heart. The emphasis is on the attitude and motivation behind the act of giving.

This verse underscores the importance of giving with a joyful and willing heart, as it is the heart's attitude that God values. It also promotes the idea that each person should give according to their own heartfelt purpose, without external pressure.

Verse 8 (2 Corinthians 9:8, KJV):

"And God is able to make all grace abound toward you; that ye, always having all sufficiency in all things, may abound to every good work:"

Expository Commentary on Verse 8:

In this verse, Paul assures the Corinthians of God's ability to provide abundantly for them in various ways.

- "And God is able to make all grace abound toward you;" - Paul emphasizes God's ability to shower the Corinthians with abundant grace. God can extend His favor and blessings toward them in a rich and overflowing manner.

- "that ye, always having all sufficiency in all things," - The result of God's abundant grace is that the Corinthians will consistently have all they need in every situation. They will experience sufficiency and provision in all areas of life.

- "may abound to every good work:" - With God's blessings and sufficiency, the Corinthians will have the capacity to excel in performing every excellent work, including acts of charity and kindness.

This verse highlights God's ability to provide generously and abundantly to His faithful followers, enabling them to engage in acts of charity and service.

Verse 9 (2 Corinthians 9:9, KJV):

"As it is written, He hath dispersed abroad; he hath given to the poor: his righteousness remaineth forever."

Expository Commentary on Verse 9:

In this verse, Paul quotes from the Old Testament to support his point about generosity and its lasting impact.

- "As it is written," - Paul references a scriptural passage to illustrate his point.

- "He hath dispersed abroad; he hath given to the poor:" - The quoted text describes the generous actions of an individual who scatters resources and gives to the poor. This is a reference to the righteous act of giving to those in need.

- "his righteousness remaineth forever." - The passage emphasizes that the righteousness of the one who gives generously endures eternally. Generous acts of charity and giving have an enduring impact and are rewarded by God.

Paul uses this Old Testament reference to reinforce the idea that giving to the poor and engaging in acts of charity is an expression of righteousness that has an eternal significance.

This section of 2 Corinthians 9 highlights the principles of generosity, cheerful giving, and the promise of God's abundance and enduring righteousness for those who engage in acts of charity and benevolence. It encourages believers to give willingly, joyfully, and abundantly, knowing that God rewards such actions.

Verse 10 (2 Corinthians 9:10, KJV):

"Now he that ministereth seed to the sower both minister bread for your food, and multiply your seed sown, and increase the fruits of your righteousness;)"

Expository Commentary on Verse 10:

In this verse, Paul continues to discuss the principles of giving and God's provision.

- "Now he that ministereth seed to the sower" - Paul refers to God as the one who provides seed to those who sow, emphasizing God's role as the ultimate source of all resources.

- "both minister bread for your food," - In addition to providing seed for sowing, God also provides sustenance and food for those who work.

- "and multiply your seed sown," - God not only provides the initial seed but also increases the yield of what is sown. This speaks to God's ability to multiply the resources of the giver.

- "and increase the fruits of your righteousness;)" - The fruits or results of the righteous act of giving are multiplied and increased by God. When individuals give generously and righteously, God blesses the outcomes and brings abundance.

This verse emphasizes that God is the ultimate source of provision and blessing. Those who give generously can trust that God will multiply their resources and increase the fruits of their righteous actions.

Verse 11 (2 Corinthians 9:11, KJV):

"Being enriched in everything to all bountifulness, which causeth through us thanksgiving to God."

Expository Commentary on Verse 11:

In this verse, Paul elaborates on the enrichment that comes through generosity and its impact.

- "Being enriched in everything to all bountifulness," - Paul explains that those who give generously are enriched in every way, not just materially but in various aspects of life. This enrichment leads to an abundance of blessings and virtuous deeds.

- "which causeth through us thanksgiving to God." - The bountifulness of those who give generously results in thanksgiving to God through the ministry of Paul and his companions. Their acts of charity and benevolence inspire gratitude and praise to God.

This verse underscores the idea that generosity leads to enrichment and abundant blessings. It also highlights the role of the giver's actions in causing others to express gratitude to God.

In these verses, Paul continues to emphasize the principles of generous giving and God's abundant provision. Believers are encouraged to sow generously, knowing that God will multiply their resources and bring blessings that lead to thanksgiving to God. The passage reflects the interconnectedness of giving, enrichment, and thanksgiving in the context of Christian charity.

Verse 12 (2 Corinthians 9:12, KJV):

"For the administration of this service not only supplieth the want of the saints, but is abundant also by many thanksgivings unto God;"

Expository Commentary on Verse 12:

In this verse, Paul continues to discuss the significance of the Corinthians' charitable service.

- "For the administration of this service" - Paul refers to the act of collecting and distributing charitable offerings for the saints in need.

- "not only supplieth the want of the saints," - The service is not merely meeting the material needs of the saints in Jerusalem but is addressing their lack or deficiency.

- "but is abundant also by many thanksgivings unto God;" - Beyond meeting the needs, this service results in an abundance of thanksgiving to God. It generates gratitude and praise to God from both the givers and the recipients.

This verse underscores that charitable service not only addresses material needs but also fosters a sense of abundance in thanksgiving to God. It highlights the spiritual and communal impact of acts of charity.

Verse 13 (2 Corinthians 9:13, KJV):

"Whiles by the experiment of this ministration they glorify God for your professed subjection unto the gospel of Christ, and for your liberal distribution unto them, and unto all men;"

Expository Commentary on Verse 13:

In this verse, Paul explains how the Corinthians' charitable service leads to the glorification of God and praise for their commitment to the gospel.

- "Whiles by the experiment of this ministration" - The act of providing for the saints in Jerusalem serves as an experiment or test.

- "they glorify God" - The result of this experiment is the glorification of God. It brings honor and praise to Him.

- "for your professed subjection unto the gospel of Christ," - The Corinthians' voluntary submission to the message and teachings of the gospel of Christ is acknowledged and celebrated.

- "and for your liberal distribution unto them, and unto all men;" - Their generous giving, not only to the saints but to all in need, is also a cause for praise and thanksgiving.

This verse highlights the positive impact of the Corinthians' charity on the perception of their commitment to the gospel and their willingness to help those in need, bringing glory to God.

Verse 14 (2 Corinthians 9:14, KJV):

"And by their prayer for you, which long after you for the exceeding grace of God in you."

Expository Commentary on Verse 14:

In this verse, Paul continues to describe the response of the saints in Jerusalem to the Corinthians' charitable service.

- "And by their prayer for you," - The saints in Jerusalem respond to the Corinthians' generosity by offering prayers on their behalf.

- "which long after you" - The saints in Jerusalem have a deep longing and affection for the Corinthians.

- "for the exceeding grace of God in you." - This longing is based on their recognition of the abundant grace of God that is evident in the Corinthians. They see the grace of God manifested in the generosity and compassion of the Corinthians.

This verse emphasizes the reciprocal relationship between the Corinthians and the saints in Jerusalem. The Corinthians' generosity leads to prayers and deep affection from the recipients, who recognize God's grace in the givers.

Verse 15 (2 Corinthians 9:15, KJV):

"Thanks be unto God for his unspeakable gift."

Expository Commentary on Verse 15:

In this final verse of 2 Corinthians 9, Paul offers a succinct expression of gratitude to God for His indescribable gift.

- "Thanks be unto God" - Paul begins by giving thanks to God.

- "for his unspeakable gift." - The reason for his gratitude is the incredible and indescribable gift that God has given. While not specified here, this gift likely refers to the gift of salvation through Jesus Christ.

This verse encapsulates the overarching theme of the chapter, which is the generosity and grace of God. It emphasizes the idea that God's gift, which is beyond words or description, is the ultimate cause for thanksgiving and praise.

In these verses, Paul underscores the spiritual and communal impact of charitable service. The Corinthians' generosity not only addresses material needs but also fosters thanksgiving to God, glorification of God, and affectionate prayers from the recipients. The chapter concludes with a profound expression of gratitude for God's incomparable gift, emphasizing the ultimate source of all blessings and grace.

Chapter 10
Authority and Spiritual Warfare

The theme of 2 Corinthians Chapter 10 is the authority and spiritual warfare of the apostle Paul, contrasting his meekness in person with his boldness in his letters. In this chapter, Paul defends his apostolic authority and addresses accusations made by some in the Corinthian church who challenged his authority and methods of ministry.

Key themes in 2 Corinthians Chapter 10 include:

1. Apostolic Authority: The central theme of this chapter is the apostolic authority of Paul. He emphasizes that his authority is from the Lord and that he is called to build up the Corinthians and edify the church.

2. Spiritual Warfare: Paul speaks of spiritual warfare, emphasizing that the weapons of his warfare are not carnal but mighty through God. He contends that his ministry involves battling against spiritual strongholds and false teachings.

3. Meekness and Boldness: Paul addresses the contrast between his meek and humble demeanor in person and the boldness of his letters. He explains that he uses boldness in his letters when addressing issues of doctrine and challenges to his authority.

4. Tearing Down Strongholds: Paul talks about pulling down strongholds and casting down arguments that exalt themselves against the knowledge of God. He aims to bring every thought into captivity to the obedience of Christ.

5. Spiritual Assessment: Paul challenges the Corinthians to assess their situation and themselves spiritually, recognizing the authenticity of his apostolic ministry and the potential consequences of not doing so.

In summary, 2 Corinthians Chapter 10 underscores the authority and spiritual warfare of the apostle Paul, his commitment to building up the church, and his defense against challenges to his authority. It also highlights the tension between meekness and boldness in his ministry and the need for spiritual assessment and discernment within the Corinthian church.

Verse 1 (2 Corinthians 10:1, KJV):

"Now I Paul myself beseech you by the meekness and gentleness of Christ, who in presence am base among you, but being absent am bold toward you:"

Expository Commentary on Verse 1:

In this verse, Paul begins by appealing to the Corinthians in the name of Christ's meekness and gentleness.

- "Now I Paul myself beseech you" - Paul emphasizes that he is personally making this appeal, underscoring the importance of his message.

- "by the meekness and gentleness of Christ," - Paul's appeal is grounded in the qualities of meekness and gentleness that characterize the nature of Christ. He wants to approach the Corinthians with the same Christ-like spirit.

- "who in presence am base among you," - Paul acknowledges that when he is physically present with the Corinthians, he may appear unimpressive or humble, possibly due to his meek and gentle demeanor.

- "but being absent am bold toward you:" - In contrast, when he is absent and writing to them, he exhibits boldness in his communication and correction.

This verse sets the tone for the following verses by highlighting Paul's intention to address the Corinthians with a balance of meekness and boldness, appealing to Christ's character as his example.

Verse 2 (2 Corinthians 10:2, KJV):

"But I beseech you, that I may not be bold when I am present with that confidence, wherewith I think to be bold against some, which think of us as if we walked according to the flesh."

Expository Commentary on Verse 2:

Paul continues his appeal, expressing his desire to avoid a confrontational and bold approach when he is physically present with the Corinthians.

- "But I beseech you, that I may not be bold when I am present with that confidence," - Paul earnestly asks the Corinthians to consider his appeal, hoping that he won't need to confront them boldly during his physical presence with the confidence he plans to display.

- "wherewith I think to be bold against some," - Paul anticipates that there will be certain individuals among the Corinthians who require a bold response due to their attitudes or actions.

- "which think of us as if we walked according to the flesh." - Paul implies that some within the Corinthian community have a negative perception of him and his fellow workers, accusing them of operating in a worldly or fleshly manner.

This verse emphasizes Paul's intention to resolve issues with the Corinthians in a manner guided by the Spirit and not to confront them harshly unless absolutely necessary.

Verse 3 (2 Corinthians 10:3, KJV):

"For though we walk in the flesh, we do not war after the flesh:"

Expository Commentary on Verse 3:

Paul now explains the nature of the spiritual conflict in which he and his co-workers are engaged.

- "For though we walk in the flesh," - Paul acknowledges that they live in human bodies and engage in earthly existence.

- "we do not war after the flesh:" - Despite living in the flesh, their spiritual battle is not conducted using fleshly or worldly means. Their conflict is spiritual and waged with spiritual weapons.

This verse underscores the distinction between the physical, earthly realm and the spiritual realm. While they live in the flesh, their battles and efforts are guided by spiritual principles and weapons.

Verse 4 (2 Corinthians 10:4, KJV):

"(For the weapons of our warfare are not carnal, but mighty through God to the pulling down of strong holds;)"

Expository Commentary on Verse 4:

Paul continues to explain the nature of the spiritual warfare and the power of their weapons.

- "(For the weapons of our warfare are not carnal," - Paul clarifies that the weapons they employ in their spiritual conflict are not of a carnal or worldly nature.

- "but mighty through God to the pulling down of strong holds;)" - Instead, their weapons are powerful through God's influence, capable of demolishing spiritual strongholds or barriers.

This verse highlights the distinction between the weapons of worldly warfare and the spiritual weapons provided by God, which are powerful for overcoming spiritual obstacles.

Verse 5 (2 Corinthians 10:5, KJV):

"Casting down imaginations, and every high thing that exalteth itself against the knowledge of God, and bringing into captivity every thought to the obedience of Christ;"

Expository Commentary on Verse 5:

Paul describes the nature of their spiritual warfare and the objectives of their efforts.

- "Casting down imaginations," - They engage in a battle that involves dismantling or tearing down human reasonings, speculations, and arguments that oppose God's truth.

- "and every high thing that exalteth itself against the knowledge of God," - Their warfare is against every proud and lofty idea or philosophy that opposes the knowledge of God, essentially anything that contradicts God's revealed truth.

- "and bringing into captivity every thought to the obedience of Christ;" - Their goal is to take every thought and mindset captive, subjecting it to the authority and obedience of Christ. This reflects the spiritual transformation of the mind.

This verse illustrates the spiritual struggle they are engaged in, which involves dismantling opposing ideologies and bringing every thought and belief under the lordship of Christ.

Verse 6 (2 Corinthians 10:6, KJV):

"And having in a readiness to revenge all disobedience, when your obedience is fulfilled."

Expository Commentary on Verse 6:

Paul concludes this section by expressing his preparedness to address disobedience.

- "And having in a readiness to revenge all disobedience," - Paul is prepared to take action and address any disobedience or rebellion within the Corinthian community.

- "when your obedience is fulfilled." - His preference is to deal with disobedience when their obedience to the truth and the gospel is complete. In other words, he hopes they will choose obedience over rebellion.

This verse reflects Paul's desire to see the Corinthians turn from disobedience to obedience and his readiness to address any issues that may hinder their spiritual growth.

In these verses, Paul presents the nature of spiritual warfare, emphasizing the use of spiritual weapons, the tearing down of opposition to God's truth, and the submission of every thought and belief to Christ's authority. Paul's goal is not only to confront disobedience but to see the Corinthians transformed into obedient followers of Christ.

Verse 7 (2 Corinthians 10:7, KJV):

"Do ye look on things after the outward appearance? If any man trust to himself that he is Christ's, let him of himself think this again, that, as he is Christ's, even so are we Christ's."

Expository Commentary on Verse 7:

In this verse, Paul addresses the Corinthians' tendency to judge based on outward appearances and their evaluation of those who claim to belong to Christ.

- "Do ye look on things after the outward appearance?" - Paul challenges the Corinthians for making judgments based on outward appearances, such as the way people present themselves or their claims to be followers of Christ.

- "If any man trust to himself that he is Christ's, let him of himself think this again," - Paul suggests that if anyone claims to be a follower of Christ and places confidence in their own identity as such, they should reconsider their perspective and reevaluate themselves.

- "that, as he is Christ's, even so are we Christ's." - Paul reminds them that just as they belong to Christ, he and his fellow apostles also belong to Christ. There is no hierarchy or superiority in being Christ's followers.

This verse addresses a potential issue of pride and self-exaltation among some in the Corinthian community, and Paul urges them to reconsider their evaluations and judgments based on outward appearances.

Verse 8 (2 Corinthians 10:8, KJV):

"For though I should boast somewhat more of our authority, which the Lord hath given us for edification, and not for your destruction, I should not be ashamed:"

Expository Commentary on Verse 8:

In this verse, Paul discusses the authority given to him by the Lord and its purpose.

- "For though I should boast somewhat more of our authority," - Paul acknowledges that he has authority as an apostle, and he has the ability to boast about it, though he doesn't do so in a self-glorifying manner.

- "which the Lord hath given us for edification," - He specifies that this authority has been granted by the Lord for the purpose of building up and strengthening the faith and spiritual growth of the Corinthians.

- "and not for your destruction," - The authority he possesses is not intended for their harm or destruction. It is meant to be a positive and constructive force.

- "I should not be ashamed:" - Paul is confident that if he were to boast about his authority, he would not feel ashamed because he uses it for edification.

This verse underscores the legitimate authority that Paul has as an apostle and his commitment to using it for the spiritual growth and edification of the Corinthian believers, rather than for destructive purposes.

Verse 9 (2 Corinthians 10:9, KJV):

"That I may not seem as if I would terrify you by letters."

Expository Commentary on Verse 9:

In this verse, Paul clarifies his intentions in writing to the Corinthians.

- "That I may not seem as if I would terrify you by letters." - Paul expresses his desire not to give the impression that his letters are intended to intimidate or frighten the Corinthians. He doesn't want them to perceive his written words as harsh or intimidating.

This verse reveals Paul's concern about the Corinthians' perception of his written communication and his desire to maintain a constructive and edifying tone in his letters.

Verse 10 (2 Corinthians 10:10, KJV):

"For his letters, say they, are weighty and powerful; but his bodily presence is weak, and his speech contemptible."

Expository Commentary on Verse 10:

In this verse, Paul references the criticism he has received from some in Corinth regarding his letters and his personal presence.

- "For his letters, say they, are weighty and powerful;" - Some in Corinth have commented that Paul's letters are strong and impactful.

- "but his bodily presence is weak, and his speech contemptible." - However, they also claim that when Paul is physically present, he appears unimpressive and his speaking ability is not highly regarded.

This verse highlights a contrast in perception between Paul's written communication and his personal presence. Some may have criticized him for appearing unimpressive in person compared to the strength of his letters.

Verse 11 (2 Corinthians 10:11, KJV):

"Let such an one think this, that, such as we are in word by letters when we are absent, such will we be also in deed when we are present."

Expository Commentary on Verse 11:

In this verse, Paul responds to the criticism and offers a clear message.

- "Let such a one think this," - Paul addresses the individual or individuals who have made these critical remarks.

- "that

, such as we are in word by letters when we are absent," - He asserts that the same strength and authority that is conveyed in his written letters will also be evident when he is absent.

- "such will we be also indeed when we are present." - In essence, Paul reassures them that his actions and behavior in person will align with the authoritative tone of his letters.

This verse emphasizes the consistency of Paul's character and ministry, whether communicated through letters or in person. He wants to dispel any doubts about his authenticity and the authority of his message.

In this section of 2 Corinthians 10, Paul addresses concerns about his authority, the power of his letters, and the contrast between his written communication and his personal presence. He emphasizes that his authority is for edification, not destruction, and that his character and ministry remain consistent, whether in writing or in person. Paul's aim is to maintain a spirit of constructive edification within the Corinthian community.

Verse 12 (2 Corinthians 10:12, KJV):

"For we dare not make ourselves of the number or compare ourselves with some that commend themselves: but they are measuring themselves by themselves, and comparing themselves among themselves, are not wise."

Expository Commentary on Verse 12:

In this verse, Paul addresses the issue of comparisons and self-promotion among individuals.

- "For we dare not make ourselves of the number," - Paul states that he and his fellow workers do not dare to include themselves among those who commend themselves, meaning they do not engage in self-promotion.

- "or compare ourselves with some that commend themselves:" - Paul refrains from comparing himself or his ministry to those who boast about their own accomplishments or status.

- "but they are measuring themselves by themselves, and comparing themselves among themselves, are not wise." - Paul criticizes those who measure their worth and success based on their own standards and by comparing themselves to others in a self-referential manner. He considers such behavior unwise.

This verse emphasizes the importance of avoiding self-centered comparisons and self-promotion. Paul promotes a humbler and Christ-centered approach to evaluating one's ministry and impact.

Verse 13 (2 Corinthians 10:13, KJV):

"But we will not boast of things without our measure, but according to the measure of the rule which God hath distributed to us, a measure to reach even unto you."

Expository Commentary on Verse 13:

In this verse, Paul clarifies his approach to boasting and the scope of his ministry.

- "But we will not boast of things without our measure," - Paul asserts that he will not boast beyond the measure or limit set for him.

- "but according to the measure of the rule which God hath distributed to us," - His boasting will align with the measure or boundary that God has assigned to him, adhering to the guidelines set by God.

- "a measure to reach even unto you." - This measure extends to include the Corinthians, meaning that his boasting and ministry are meant to encompass them.

Paul is careful to align his ministry and boasting with God's appointed measure, which includes reaching out to the Corinthians.

Verse 14 (2 Corinthians 10:14, KJV):

"For we stretch not ourselves beyond our measure, as though we reached not unto you: for we are come as far as to you also in preaching the gospel of Christ:"

Expository Commentary on Verse 14:

Paul continues to emphasize that his ministry aligns with the appointed measure and the scope of his mission.

- "For we stretch not ourselves beyond our measure," - Paul reiterates that he does not overextend his ministry beyond the boundaries God has set for him.

- "as though we reached not unto you:" - He clarifies that his ministry does reach and include the Corinthians.

- "for we are come as far as to you also in preaching the gospel of Christ:" - He affirms that he has indeed reached them with the message of the gospel of Christ.

This verse emphasizes the accuracy of Paul's ministry and his faithfulness in carrying the gospel to the Corinthians as part of the appointed measure.

Verse 15 (2 Corinthians 10:15, KJV):

"Not boasting of things without our measure, that is, of other men's labours; but having hope, when your faith is increased, that we shall be enlarged by you according to our rule abundantly,"

Expository Commentary on Verse 15:

Paul continues to address his approach to boasting and ministry.

- "Not boasting of things without our measure," - Paul reiterates that he does not engage in boasting beyond the appointed measure, specifically by claiming the work of others as his own.

- "that is, of other men's labours;" - He clarifies that he does not boast about the labors or achievements of others, which would be beyond his measure.

- "but having hope, when your faith is increased," - Instead of boasting in others' work, Paul expresses hope and anticipation. He looks forward to a time when the faith of the Corinthians will grow and increase.

- "that we shall be enlarged by you according to our rule abundantly," - His hope is that as the Corinthians' faith expands, they will also contribute to his ministry according to the rule or measure set by God, resulting in an abundant and fruitful ministry.

This verse underscores Paul's commitment to operating within the boundaries set by God and his expectation that the Corinthians' growth in faith will lead to a mutually beneficial ministry.

Verse 16 (2 Corinthians 10:16, KJV):

"To preach the gospel in the regions beyond you, and not to boast in another man's line of things made ready to our hand."

Expository Commentary on Verse 16:

In this verse, Paul explains his broader mission and intentions.

- "To preach the gospel in the regions beyond you," - Paul's primary aim is to continue preaching the gospel in areas that extend beyond the Corinthian community.

- "and not to boast in another man's line of things made ready to our hand." - He clarifies that his purpose is not to boast about work that others have already accomplished. He seeks to focus on the mission of preaching the gospel in unreached areas.

This verse highlights Paul's dedication to expanding the reach of the gospel and his desire to avoid boasting in the work done by others.

Verse 17 (2 Corinthians 10:17, KJV):

"But he that glorieth, let him glory in the Lord."

Expository Commentary on Verse 17:

Paul concludes this section by emphasizing where true glory or boasting should be directed.

- "But he that glorieth, let him glory in the Lord." - Paul's instruction is clear: if anyone boasts or glories, their focus should be on the Lord. True and rightful boasting should be in the Lord and His work, rather than in human achievements or self-promotion.

This verse underscores the importance of giving all glory and praise to the Lord, recognizing that He is the source of all accomplishments and blessings.

Verse 18 (2 Corinthians 10:18, KJV):

"For not he that commendeth himself is approved, but whom the Lord commendeth."

Expository Commentary on Verse 18:

Paul concludes this section by highlighting the source of approval and commendation.

- "For not he that commendeth himself is approved," - Paul points out that self-commendation or self-praise is not the basis for approval or commendation.

- "but whom the Lord commendeth." - True approval and commendation come from the Lord. It is God's assessment that ultimately matters.

This verse emphasizes the need for humility and reliance on God's evaluation and commendation rather than self-promotion.

In this section of 2 Corinthians 10, Paul addresses issues related to boasting, comparisons, and the boundaries of his ministry. He underscores the importance of aligning with the measure set by God, avoiding self-promotion, and directing all glory to the Lord. Paul's focus is on the expansion of the gospel and the commendation that comes from the Lord rather than human praise.

Chapter 11
Apostle Paul's Authority

The theme of 2 Corinthians Chapter 11 primarily centers around the defense of the apostle Paul's apostolic authority, his concern for the spiritual well-being of the Corinthians, and the exposure of false apostles who were misleading the Corinthian church. This chapter serves as a passionate and forceful defense of Paul's legitimacy as an apostle and highlights the dangers of false teachings and deceptive leaders.

Key themes in 2 Corinthians Chapter 11 include:

1. Apostolic Authority: Paul vigorously defends his authority as an apostle of Christ. He points out that he has the same calling and commission as the "super-apostles" who were influencing the Corinthians, and he affirms his credentials.

2. Spiritual Deception: The chapter highlights the danger of spiritual deception. Paul is deeply concerned that the Corinthians are being led astray by false apostles who preach a different gospel. He warns about the subtlety of Satan's influence in spreading false teachings.

3. Self-Sacrifice and Suffering: Paul describes his own hardships, sufferings, and sacrifices in ministry to emphasize the genuineness of his calling and his love for the Corinthian church.

4. Spiritual Warfare: The chapter touches on the concept of spiritual warfare. Paul describes the challenges and opposition he has faced

in his ministry and underscores the need for vigilance against false teachings.

5. Love and Concern for the Corinthians: Despite the confrontational tone of the chapter, it reveals Paul's deep love and concern for the spiritual well-being of the Corinthians. He fears that they are being led astray and passionately seeks to protect and guide them in the truth.

6. Boasting in Weakness: Paul alludes to the paradox of boasting in weakness, similar to themes explored in other chapters of 2 Corinthians. He acknowledges his own weaknesses and limitations but emphasizes the power of Christ in his life and ministry.

In summary, 2 Corinthians Chapter 11 is a powerful and emotional defense of Paul's apostolic authority and a warning against the influence of false apostles and their misleading teachings. It underscores the importance of discernment, the genuineness of apostolic ministry, and the need to remain faithful to the true gospel of Christ in the face of spiritual deception.

Verse 1 (2 Corinthians 11:1, KJV):

"Would to God ye could bear with me a little in my folly: and indeed bear with me."

Expository Commentary on Verse 1:

In this verse, Paul begins with a heartfelt plea to the Corinthians.

- "Would to God ye could bear with me a little in my folly:" - Paul expresses his wish that the Corinthians would indulge him for a brief moment as he speaks somewhat "foolishly." This is a rhetorical device to capture their attention, as what he's about to say may seem unconventional.

- "and indeed bear with me." - He reiterates his plea for them to bear with him. This underscores his desire for their patience and willingness to listen.

Paul's tone in this verse is one of affection and earnestness. He is preparing to say something important, and he asks for their patience and understanding.

Verse 2 (2 Corinthians 11:2, KJV):

"For I am jealous over you with godly jealousy: for I have espoused you to one husband, that I may present you as a chaste virgin to Christ."

Expository Commentary on Verse 2:

In this verse, Paul expresses his deep concern and care for the Corinthians.

- "For I am jealous over you with godly jealousy:" - Paul uses the term "jealous" to convey his protective and loving concern for the spiritual well-being of the Corinthians. This jealousy is not rooted in selfishness but is "godly," indicating his desire for their spiritual purity and faithfulness.

- "for I have espoused you to one husband," - Paul uses the metaphor of marriage to describe the spiritual relationship between the Corinthians and Christ. He sees himself as the one who has brought them into this relationship.

- "that I may present you as a chaste virgin to Christ." - Paul's goal is to present the Corinthians to Christ as a pure and faithful bride, untarnished by false teachings or spiritual unfaithfulness.

This verse underscores Paul's deep love and concern for the spiritual well-being of the Corinthians. He is like a spiritual father or guardian who desires to see them remain faithful to their relationship with Christ.

Verse 3 (2 Corinthians 11:3, KJV):

"But I fear, lest by any means, as the serpent beguiled Eve through his subtilty, so your minds should be corrupted from the simplicity that is in Christ."

Expository Commentary on Verse 3:

In this verse, Paul expresses his fear of a potential spiritual danger.

- "But I fear, lest by any means," - Paul is concerned and apprehensive about what he's about to describe.

- "as the serpent beguiled Eve through his subtilty," - He draws a parallel to the way the serpent (Satan) deceived Eve in the Garden of Eden through cunning and deception. He sees a similar potential for deception in the Corinthian community.

- "so your minds should be corrupted from the simplicity that is in Christ." - His fear is that just as Eve was led astray from the simple and pure devotion to God, the Corinthians might be led away from the straightforward and uncomplicated faith in Christ.

This verse highlights the ever-present spiritual threat of deception and encourages the Corinthians to maintain a genuine and uncomplicated faith in Christ.

Verse 4 (2 Corinthians 11:4, KJV):

"For if he that cometh preacheth another Jesus, whom we have not preached, or if ye receive another spirit, which ye have not received, or another gospel, which ye have not accepted, ye might well bear with him."

Expository Commentary on Verse 4:

In this verse, Paul addresses the danger of false teachings and alternative versions of the gospel.

- "For if he that cometh preacheth another Jesus, whom we have not preached," - Paul warns against the introduction of a distorted or false version of Jesus, different from the authentic Jesus he and the apostles have preached.

- "or if ye receive another spirit, which ye have not received," - He cautions the Corinthians not to embrace a different, counterfeit, or misleading spirit that contrasts with the Holy Spirit they have received.

- "or another gospel, which ye have not accepted," - Paul emphasizes the importance of adhering to the true gospel message they have accepted, as opposed to accepting a counterfeit or distorted version.

- "ye might well bear with him." - Paul expresses his concern that the Corinthians are accommodating and tolerating those who preach a false gospel or a different version of Christ.

This verse underscores the need for discernment and a commitment to the authentic gospel and teachings of Christ, as opposed to being swayed by deceptive or counterfeit versions of the faith.

In these verses, Paul conveys his deep concern for the Corinthians' spiritual well-being, likening himself to a protective guardian of their faith. He warns against the potential for deception and the acceptance of distorted versions of the gospel or Christ, urging them to remain

faithful to the simplicity of their faith in Christ. His words serve as a cautionary message to guard against spiritual deception and false teachings.

Verse 5 (2 Corinthians 11:5, KJV):

"For I suppose I was not a whit behind the very chiefest apostles."

Expository Commentary on Verse 5:

In this verse, Paul defends his apostolic authority and position.

- "For I suppose I was not a whit behind the very chiefest apostles." - Paul asserts that he does not consider himself inferior to the most prominent apostles, indicating that he believes he stands on equal footing with them in terms of his apostolic authority.

This verse reflects Paul's determination to establish his legitimacy as an apostle and to counter any doubts or criticisms regarding his status.

Verse 6 (2 Corinthians 11:6, KJV):

"But though I be rude in speech, yet not in knowledge; but we have been throughly made manifest among you in all things."

Expository Commentary on Verse 6:

In this verse, Paul addresses the perception of his speaking abilities and the depth of his knowledge.

- "But though I be rude in speech," - Paul acknowledges that some may have criticized his style of speaking, perhaps considering it less eloquent or polished.

- "yet not in knowledge;" - He affirms that his knowledge and understanding of the gospel and spiritual matters are not lacking. Despite any perceived limitations in his speech, his understanding and insight are substantial.

- "but we have been throughly made manifest among you in all things." - Paul assures the Corinthians that he and his message have been clearly and completely revealed to them in every aspect. His authenticity and teachings have been thoroughly demonstrated.

This verse underscores that Paul's authority and knowledge are not dependent on eloquence of speech, but on the depth of his understanding and the manifest evidence of his ministry among the Corinthians.

Verse 7 (2 Corinthians 11:7, KJV):

"Have I committed an offence in abasing myself that ye might be exalted, because I have preached to you the gospel of God freely?"

Expository Commentary on Verse 7:

In this verse, Paul questions whether he has done wrong by humbling himself for the benefit of the Corinthians.

- "Have I committed an offence in abasing myself that ye might be exalted," - Paul asks whether he has made a mistake by humbling himself, perhaps by not seeking financial support or by presenting himself in a self-effacing manner, all for the purpose of elevating the Corinthians.

- "because I have preached to you the gospel of God freely?" - He explains that his motive for this self-abasement is to ensure that he has preached the gospel of God to them without seeking material gain or compensation.

Paul's questioning in this verse is a rhetorical device to make the Corinthians reflect on the sincerity of his motives.

Verse 8 (2 Corinthians 11:8, KJV):

"I robbed other churches, taking wages of them, to do you service."

Expository Commentary on Verse 8:

In this verse, Paul explains his financial support in more detail.

- "I robbed other churches, taking wages of them," - Paul clarifies that he received financial support from other churches to be able to serve the Corinthians. This support was not robbery in the criminal sense but refers to him receiving financial assistance from other congregations.

- "to do you service." - He emphasizes that the financial support he received from other churches was used to enable him to serve the Corinthians, ensuring that he was not a financial burden to them.

This verse highlights Paul's commitment to providing the Corinthians with his ministry while avoiding imposing financial obligations on them.

Verse 9 (2 Corinthians 11:9, KJV):

"And when I was present with you, and wanted, I was chargeable to no man: for that which was lacking to me the brethren which came from Macedonia supplied: and in all things I have kept myself from being burdensome unto you, and so will I keep myself."

Expository Commentary on Verse 9:

In this verse, Paul continues to explain his financial approach while present with the Corinthians.

- "And when I was present with you, and wanted," - Paul refers to his physical presence with the Corinthians when he experienced needs or material lack.

- "I was chargeable to no man:" - He underscores that he did not become a financial burden to anyone in the Corinthian community.

- "for that which was lacking to me the brethren which came from Macedonia supplied:" - He clarifies that the financial needs he had were met by contributions from the brethren who came from Macedonia, allowing him to avoid seeking support from the Corinthians.

- "and in all things I have kept myself from being burdensome unto you, and so will I keep myself." - Paul reaffirms his commitment to not burden the Corinthians financially, indicating that he will continue this practice in the future.

This verse illustrates Paul's dedication to providing his ministry to the Corinthians without placing a financial weight on them.

Verse 10 (2 Corinthians 11:10, KJV):

"As the truth of Christ is in me, no man shall stop me of this boasting in the regions of Achaia."

Expository Commentary on Verse 10:

In this verse, Paul vows to maintain his approach to financial matters as a point of pride in the regions of Achaia.

- "As the truth of Christ is in me," - Paul invokes the truth of Christ within him as a witness to the sincerity of his words and intentions.

- "no man shall stop me of this boasting in the regions of Achaia." - He declares his determination to continue his practice of not seeking financial support from the Corinthians as a matter of boasting in the regions of Achaia (the broader area where Corinth was located).

This verse demonstrates Paul's unwavering commitment to his approach in the matter of financial support, emphasizing that no one will deter him from this practice in the regions of Achaia.

Verse 11 (2 Corinthians 11:11, KJV):

"Wherefore? because I love you not? God knoweth."

Expository Commentary on Verse 11:

In this verse, Paul responds to any potential doubts about his motives.

- "Wherefore? because I love you not?" - Paul raises the question of whether his refusal to seek financial support from the Corinthians is an indication of his lack of love for them.

- "God knoweth." - He leaves the answer to God, indicating that God knows the sincerity of his love for the Corinthians.

This verse underscores that Paul's motives are rooted in love, and he leaves the judgment of his heart to God, who knows his true intentions.

In this section of 2 Corinthians 11, Paul defends his apostolic authority, addresses questions about his financial support, and emphasizes his love and commitment to the Corinthians. His words are intended to demonstrate the sincerity of his ministry and his dedication to serving them selflessly.

Verse 12 (2 Corinthians 11:12, KJV):

"But what I do, that I will do, that I may cut off occasion from them which desire occasion; that wherein they glory, they may be found even as we."

Expository Commentary on Verse 12:

In this verse, Paul reaffirms his commitment to a specific course of action.

- "But what I do, that I will do," - Paul is resolute in his decision, emphasizing that he will continue to act in a certain way.

- "that I may cut off occasion from them which desire occasion;" - He explains that his purpose is to eliminate any opportunity for those who seek to find fault or accuse him. By maintaining his chosen course of action, he aims to deprive his critics of any legitimate grounds for criticism.

- "that wherein they glory, they may be found even as we." - Paul's intent is to expose the hypocrisy of his opponents who boast or glory in their own actions. He wants them to be seen in a similar light to himself.

This verse reflects Paul's determination to act in a way that maintains his integrity and reveals the true character of those who oppose him.

Verse 13 (2 Corinthians 11:13, KJV):

"For such are false apostles, deceitful workers, transforming themselves into the apostles of Christ."

Expository Commentary on Verse 13:

In this verse, Paul provides a scathing description of his opponents.

- "For such are false apostles," - Paul characterizes them as counterfeit or deceitful apostles, implying that they do not possess the authentic authority and mission of true apostles.

- "deceitful workers," - He further labels them as deceptive laborers, suggesting that their actions are characterized by deception and dishonesty.

- "transforming themselves into the apostles of Christ." - He accuses them of masquerading as genuine apostles of Christ, implying that they are impostors.

This verse serves to unmask those who oppose Paul as false apostles and deceitful workers who pretend to be genuine messengers of Christ.

Verse 14 (2 Corinthians 11:14, KJV):

"And no marvel; for Satan himself is transformed into an angel of light."

Expository Commentary on Verse 14:

In this verse, Paul explains the deceptive nature of Satan.

- "And no marvel;" - Paul implies that it should not be surprising or astonishing.

- "for Satan himself is transformed into an angel of light." - He compares the deceptive tactics of his opponents to the way Satan can present himself as an angel of light. This means that just as Satan can appear to be righteous and pure, so can Paul's adversaries disguise their true nature with a façade of righteousness.

This verse emphasizes the cunning and deceptive nature of both Paul's opponents and Satan, who can use appearances to deceive.

Verse 15 (2 Corinthians 11:15, KJV):

"Therefore, it is no great thing if his ministers also be transformed as the ministers of righteousness; whose end shall be according to their works."

Expository Commentary on Verse 15:

In this verse, Paul concludes his warning about the deceptive nature of his adversaries.

- "Therefore, it is no great thing if his ministers also be transformed as the ministers of righteousness;" - Paul suggests that it should not be considered remarkable if Satan's ministers (his opponents) also disguise themselves as ministers of righteousness. He implies that this is a tactic used by those who serve the devil.

- "whose end shall be according to their works." - He emphasizes that the ultimate judgment and destiny of these deceivers will be based on their actions and works.

This verse underscores the importance of discerning the true nature of ministers and leaders, as their ultimate fate will be determined by their deeds.

In this section of 2 Corinthians 11, Paul confronts the deceptive practices of his adversaries, characterizing them as false apostles and deceitful workers. He also draws a parallel between their tactics and the deceptive nature of Satan, highlighting the need for discernment. Paul emphasizes that the judgment of these deceivers will be based on their works, underscoring the importance of genuine righteousness and integrity in ministry.

Verse 16 (2 Corinthians 11:16, KJV):

"I say again, Let no man think me a fool; if otherwise, yet as a fool receive me, that I may boast myself a little."

Expository Commentary on Verse 16:

In this verse, Paul continues his defense and addresses those who may consider him a fool for boasting.

- "I say again, Let no man think me a fool;" - Paul repeats his request, asking that no one regard him as a fool. He's aware that his words might be perceived as boasting and seeks understanding.

- "if otherwise, yet as a fool receive me," - Even if they see him as a fool, he asks them to receive him and his words with patience and humility.

- "that I may boast myself a little." - Paul intends to engage in some self-promotion or boasting to make a point. He asks for their indulgence.

This verse reveals Paul's awareness of how he might be perceived but underscores his intention to make an important point through a form of rhetorical boasting.

Verse 17 (2 Corinthians 11:17, KJV):

"That which I speak, I speak it not after the Lord, but as it were foolishly, in this confidence of boasting."

Expository Commentary on Verse 17:

In this verse, Paul clarifies the nature of his speech and boasts.

- "That which I speak, I speak it not after the Lord," - Paul acknowledges that his manner of speech and boasting is not in strict accordance with the teachings of the Lord, as it involves self-promotion and rhetorical strategies.

- "but as it were foolishly, in this confidence of boasting." - He characterizes his speech as somewhat foolish, indicating that his confident boasting is a rhetorical device and not an expression of personal pride.

This verse reinforces the idea that Paul's boasting serves a specific purpose and is not an expression of arrogance.

Verse 18 (2 Corinthians 11:18, KJV):

"Seeing that many glory after the flesh, I will glory also."

Expository Commentary on Verse 18:

In this verse, Paul justifies his boasting by pointing out that others engage in similar behavior.

- "Seeing that much glory after the flesh," - Paul observes that many people engage in boasting based on their earthly or fleshly accomplishments and status.

- "I will glory also." - In response, he determines to engage in a form of boasting himself.

This verse highlights Paul's recognition that boasting is a common practice and that he is not alone in doing so.

Verse 19 (2 Corinthians 11:19, KJV):

"For ye suffer fools gladly, seeing ye yourselves are wise."

Expository Commentary on Verse 19:

In this verse, Paul draws attention to the Corinthians' readiness to tolerate or bear with foolish individuals.

- "For ye suffer fools gladly," - He points out that the Corinthians are willing to tolerate or put up with those who act foolishly or engage in boastful behavior.

- "seeing ye yourselves are wise." - He acknowledges that they consider themselves to be wise or knowledgeable.

Paul's statement here highlights the Corinthian's capacity to tolerate different types of behavior, including foolishness, but he is about to challenge them on this point.

Verse 20 (2 Corinthians 11:20, KJV):

"For ye suffer, if a man bring you into bondage, if a man devour you, if a man take of you, if a man exalt himself, if a man smite you on the face."

Expository Commentary on Verse 20:

In this verse, Paul criticizes the Corinthians for their tolerance of various negative behaviors.

- "For ye suffer, if a man bring you into bondage," - Paul points out that the Corinthians are willing to endure if someone enslaves or restricts them in some way.

- "if a man devour you," - He highlights their willingness to endure if someone exploits or consumes their resources.

- "if a man take of you," - He notes their endurance when someone takes from them, likely referring to financial exploitation.

- "if a man exalt himself," - Paul draws attention to their tolerance of someone who exalts or promotes themselves, even if it's done arrogantly.

- "if a man smite you on the face." - He highlights their patience even if someone physically assaults or mistreats them.

This verse underscores Paul's criticism of the Corinthians for their apparent tolerance of various negative behaviors and their willingness to endure mistreatment.

Verse 21 (2 Corinthians 11:21, KJV):

"I speak as concerning reproach, as though we had been weak. Howbeit whereinsoever any is bold, (I speak foolishly,) I am bold also."

Expository Commentary on Verse 21:

In this verse, Paul addresses the idea of reproach or criticism.

- "I speak as concerning reproach, as though we had been weak." - Paul acknowledges

that he is speaking in terms of the reproach he has endured, as if he and his associates had been weak or deficient.

- "Howbeit whereinsoever any is bold, (I speak foolishly,) I am bold also." - He qualifies that even in the areas where others boast boldly, he is willing to do the same, although he characterizes this as a form of rhetorical foolishness.

This verse emphasizes Paul's willingness to engage in rhetorical tactics to respond to criticism and to counter the boasting of his opponents.

In this section of 2 Corinthians 11, Paul addresses the issue of boasting and reproach. He acknowledges that he is engaging in a form of rhetorical self-promotion and explains the purpose behind it. He also criticizes the Corinthians for their tolerance of negative behaviors while highlighting his own willingness to match the boldness of others. Paul's words are part of his broader defense and argumentation in this letter.

Verse 22 (2 Corinthians 11:22, KJV):

"Are they Hebrews? so am I. Are they Israelites? so am I. Are they the seed of Abraham? so am I."

Expository Commentary on Verse 22:

In this verse, Paul presents his credentials and highlights his Jewish heritage in response to his opponents.

- "Are they Hebrews? so am I." - Paul asserts that he, too, is a Hebrew, which is a significant marker of his Jewish identity.

- "Are they Israelites? so am I." - He emphasizes that, like his opponents, he is an Israelite, a term denoting his lineage from the patriarch Jacob.

- "Are they the seed of Abraham? so am I." - Paul further emphasizes his Jewish ancestry by claiming to be a descendant of Abraham, the father of the Jewish nation.

This verse serves to establish Paul's Jewish heritage and background, putting him on equal footing with his opponents in terms of Jewish identity.

Verse 23 (2 Corinthians 11:23, KJV):

"Are they ministers of Christ? (I speak as a fool) I am more; in labours more abundant, in stripes above measure, in prisons more frequent, in deaths oft."

Expository Commentary on Verse 23:

In this verse, Paul asserts his qualifications as a minister of Christ and highlights his extraordinary experiences and hardships.

- "Are they ministers of Christ?" - Paul acknowledges that his opponents are also considered ministers or servants of Christ, though he regards this acknowledgment as somewhat foolish within the context of his boasting.

- "(I speak as a fool) I am more;" - Paul, using a form of rhetorical boasting, claims to be even more accomplished or experienced as a minister of Christ.

- "in labours more abundant," - He first lists his intense efforts and hard work in the service of Christ, indicating that he has labored extensively.

- "in stripes above measure," - He notes that he has endured severe floggings and physical punishments beyond measure, signifying the extent of his sufferings.

- "in prisons more frequent," - Paul emphasizes that he has been imprisoned more often than his opponents, indicating a history of incarceration.

- "in deaths oft." - He claims to have faced death multiple times in the course of his ministry, likely referring to the many life-threatening situations he encountered.

This verse underscores the remarkable sacrifices and hardships Paul has endured in his service to Christ, far surpassing those of his adversaries.

Verse 24 (2 Corinthians 11:24, KJV):

"Of the Jews five times received I forty stripes save one."

Expository Commentary on Verse 24:

In this verse, Paul provides a specific example of the hardships he endured, emphasizing the severe floggings he received from fellow Jews.

- "Of the Jews five times received I forty stripes save one." - Paul recounts that on five occasions, he endured the punishment of receiving forty lashes minus one, as prescribed by Jewish law. This punishment was a form of severe physical flogging and was incredibly painful.

This verse highlights the intensity of the physical suffering Paul endured, often at the hands of his own countrymen.

Verse 25 (2 Corinthians 11:25, KJV):

"Thrice was I beaten with rods, once was I stoned, thrice I suffered shipwreck, a night and a day I have been in the deep."

Expository Commentary on Verse 25:

In this verse, Paul continues to list the hardships he faced in his ministry, including physical beatings, stoning, and maritime disasters.

- "Thrice was I beaten with rods," - Paul endured being beaten with rods on three separate occasions. This form of punishment was a brutal and painful physical abuse.

- "once was I stoned," - He recalls being stoned once, which was a life-threatening event where he was pelted with stones by an angry mob.

- "thrice I suffered shipwreck," - Paul mentions three instances where he experienced the traumatic event of shipwreck.

- "a night and a day I have been in the deep." - He highlights that he spent a whole night and day adrift in the open sea after one of these shipwrecks.

This verse emphasizes the perilous nature of Paul's ministry, including physical violence and life-threatening situations.

Verse 26 (2 Corinthians 11:26, KJV):

"In journeyings often, in perils of waters, in perils of robbers, in perils by mine own countrymen, in perils by the heathen, in perils in the city, in perils in the wilderness, in perils in the sea, in perils among false brethren."

Expository Commentary on Verse 26:

In this verse, Paul details various dangers and perils he encountered throughout his journeys and ministry.

- "In journeyings often," - He frequently traveled in the course of his ministry, which often involved its own set of risks and challenges.

- "in perils of waters," - He faced danger while crossing bodies of water, likely referring to river crossings or sea voyages.

- "in perils of robbers," - Paul was at risk of encountering robbers or bandits during his journeys.

- "in perils by mine own countrymen," - Even his fellow Jews posed a threat to him at times, reflecting the hostility he faced from some within his own nation.

- "in perils by the heathen," - Non-Jewish, or Gentile, populations also posed dangers to Paul and his ministry.

- "in perils in the city," - Urban environments were not without danger, and Paul encountered peril in cities.

- "in perils in the wilderness," - He was exposed to dangers in desolate and uninhabited areas.

- "in perils in the sea," - Shipwrecks and maritime dangers added to the perils he faced.

- "in perils among false brethren

." - Paul had to contend with the treachery of those who falsely claimed to be fellow believers but proved to be untrustworthy.

This verse serves to illustrate the multifaceted nature of the dangers and perils Paul faced during his ministry.

Verse 27 (2 Corinthians 11:27, KJV):

"In weariness and painfulness, in watchings often, in hunger and thirst, in fastings often, in cold and nakedness."

Expository Commentary on Verse 27:

In this verse, Paul describes the physical and emotional hardships he experienced in his ministry.

- "In weariness and painfulness," - Paul endured extreme fatigue and physical pain due to the demands of his ministry.

- "in watchings often," - He had many sleepless nights, possibly due to concerns for the churches or personal hardships.

- "in hunger and thirst," - Paul experienced periods of intense hunger and thirst, likely due to a lack of provisions or persecution.

- "in fastings often," - He frequently engaged in voluntary fasting as a form of spiritual discipline.

- "in cold and nakedness." - Paul faced exposure to the elements and inadequate clothing, making him vulnerable to the cold.

This verse underscores the physical and emotional toll that Paul's ministry had on him, including deprivation and discomfort.

Verse 28 (2 Corinthians 11:28, KJV):

"Beside those things that are without, that which cometh upon me daily, the care of all the churches."

Expository Commentary on Verse 28:

In this verse, Paul mentions a particular burden that he carries daily in addition to the external hardships.

- "Beside those things that are without," - In addition to the external challenges he has mentioned.

- "that which cometh upon me daily," - Paul refers to a daily concern or burden that he carries.

- "the care of all the churches." - This daily burden is the responsibility and care for all the churches he has established or oversees. Paul feels the weight of the spiritual well-being and needs of the various congregations he has planted.

This verse highlights the heavy responsibility Paul carries for the spiritual welfare of the churches he has founded, which is an ongoing concern that adds to the burdens he faces.

Verse 29 (2 Corinthians 11:29, KJV):

"Who is weak, and I am not weak? who is offended, and I burn not?"

Expository Commentary on Verse 29:

In this verse, Paul reveals his deep empathy and concern for the struggles of others.

- "Who is weak, and I am not weak?" - Paul shows his solidarity with those who are weak or struggling, indicating that he shares in their weaknesses and vulnerabilities.

- "who is offended, and I burn not?" - He expresses his passion and indignation when someone is caused offense or harm, showing his deep care for their well-being.

This verse demonstrates Paul's empathetic and caring nature, as he is deeply affected by the difficulties and suffering of others within the Christian community.

In this section of 2 Corinthians 11, Paul provides a detailed account of the hardships and challenges he faced in his ministry. He emphasizes his Jewish heritage and qualifications as a minister of Christ, highlighting the severe physical and emotional trials he endured. Paul also underlines his daily concern for the well-being of the churches he has established. These verses serve to validate his apostolic authority and his commitment to the cause of Christ.

Verse 30 (2 Corinthians 11:30, KJV):

"If I must need glory, I will glory of the things which concern mine infirmities."

Expository Commentary on Verse 30:

In this verse, Paul continues to address the theme of boasting but with a different focus.

- "If I must need glory," - Paul acknowledges the necessity or inevitability of boasting, but he wants to direct it towards a specific aspect.

- "I will glory of the things which concern mine infirmities." - Instead of boasting about his achievements or spiritual experiences, Paul chooses to boast about his weaknesses, limitations, and physical infirmities. He emphasizes that he will take pride in the challenges and difficulties he has faced in his service to Christ.

This verse underscores a shift in Paul's approach to boasting, as he emphasizes his vulnerability and dependence on Christ, rather than his accomplishments.

Verse 31 (2 Corinthians 11:31, KJV):

"The God and Father of our Lord Jesus Christ, which is blessed for evermore, knoweth that I lie not."

Expository Commentary on Verse 31:

In this verse, Paul calls upon God as a witness to the truthfulness of his statements.

- "The God and Father of our Lord Jesus Christ," - Paul identifies God as the Father of Jesus Christ, emphasizing the divine nature of the God he serves.

- "which is blessed for evermore," - He acknowledges God's eternal blessedness and goodness.

- "knoweth that I lie not." - Paul appeals to the omniscience of God, stating that God knows he is not lying in his previous declarations and boasts.

This verse is a solemn affirmation of the truth of Paul's words and his sincerity in what he has communicated to the Corinthians.

Verse 32 (2 Corinthians 11:32, KJV):

"In Damascus the governor under Aretas the king kept the city of the Damascenes with a garrison, desirous to apprehend me:"

Expository Commentary on Verse 32:

In this verse, Paul provides a specific example of a perilous situation he encountered.

- "In Damascus the governor under Aretas the king," - Paul mentions the city of Damascus and its governor, who was under the authority of King Aretas. This would have been during his early days as a Christian.

- "kept the city of the Damascenes with a garrison," - The governor had placed a military garrison in Damascus, indicating a fortified presence.

- "desirous to apprehend me:" - This garrison was actively seeking to capture and arrest Paul, making his stay in Damascus a dangerous one.

This verse recounts a specific incident in which Paul was in grave danger, hunted by authorities in Damascus.

Verse 33 (2 Corinthians 11:33, KJV):

"And through a window in a basket was I let down by the wall, and escaped his hands."

Expository Commentary on Verse 33:

In this verse, Paul describes how he managed to escape from the governor's pursuit.

- "And through a window in a basket was I let down by the wall," - Paul was lowered in a basket through a window in the city wall. This was a dramatic escape plan that was executed to ensure his safety.

- "and escaped his hands." - The result of this escape was that he successfully evaded capture by the governor and his forces.

This verse highlights the lengths to which Paul had to go to evade capture in Damascus, a daring escape that allowed him to continue his ministry.

In this section of 2 Corinthians 11, Paul focuses on his willingness to boast about his weaknesses and infirmities, shifting away from the traditional forms of boasting. He calls upon God as a witness to the truthfulness of his statements and provides a specific example of a perilous situation in Damascus where he had to escape through a window in a basket to avoid capture. This passage further underscores the challenges and dangers Paul faced in his dedication to spreading the message of Christ.

Chapter 12
Boasting in Weakness, and the sufficiency of God's Grace

The theme of 2 Corinthians Chapter 12 revolves around the concept of weakness, boasting in weakness, and the sufficiency of God's grace. In this chapter, the apostle Paul shares his subjective experiences, including a vision of heaven and a thorn in the flesh, to illustrate the importance of recognizing one's limitations and relying on God's grace and strength.

Key themes in 2 Corinthians Chapter 12 include:

1. Boasting in Weakness: Paul begins the chapter by speaking of a vision he had of paradise but then transitions to his thorn in the flesh, which humbled him. He highlights the idea of boasting in weakness, emphasizing that God's power is made perfect in human weakness.

2. Sufficiency of God's Grace: The chapter underscores the sufficiency of God's grace to sustain believers in their weaknesses and trials. Paul acknowledges that when he is weak, he is strong through Christ's grace.

3. Visions and Revelations: Paul's reference to visions and revelations, including the vision of paradise, sheds light on the mystical experiences he had. These experiences are presented as an aspect of his ministry and relationship with God.

4. Thorn in the Flesh: Paul speaks of a "thorn in the flesh" that he had, which caused him distress. The nature of this thorn is not specified, but it serves to remind believers that even the apostle Paul faced challenges and limitations.

5. Spiritual Humility: The chapter conveys the importance of spiritual humility and dependence on God. Paul's acknowledgment of his own weaknesses and his reliance on God's grace set an example for believers.

In summary, 2 Corinthians Chapter 12 focuses on the paradox of boasting in weakness and the sufficiency of God's grace. It encourages believers to recognize their limitations, rely on God's strength, and find solace in the knowledge that His grace sustains them, even in the midst of trials and challenges.

Verse 1 (2 Corinthians 12:1, KJV):

"It is not expedient for me doubtless to glory. I will come to visions and revelations of the Lord."

Expository Commentary on Verse 1:

In this verse, Paul introduces the topic of visions and revelations he received from the Lord.

- "It is not expedient for me doubtless to glory." - Paul begins by acknowledging that boasting is not profitable or necessary. He hesitates to boast but feels compelled to share a specific experience.

- "I will come to visions and revelations of the Lord." - Paul intends to recount extraordinary spiritual experiences he had, such as visions and revelations granted to him directly by the Lord. These experiences are not common and deserve special attention.

This verse sets the stage for Paul's discussion of a remarkable spiritual encounter.

Verse 2 (2 Corinthians 12:2, KJV):

"I knew a man in Christ above fourteen years ago, (whether in the body, I cannot tell; or whether out of the body, I cannot tell: God knoweth;) such an one caught up to the third heaven."

Expository Commentary on Verse 2:

In this verse, Paul describes a transcendent experience that took place over fourteen years ago.

- "I knew a man in Christ above fourteen years ago," - Paul begins by using a form of self-reference but speaks in the third person, possibly to avoid undue self-promotion or to emphasize the objectivity of the experience. This experience occurred more than fourteen years prior to the writing of this letter.

- "(whether in the body, I cannot tell; or whether out of the body, I cannot tell: God knoweth;)" - Paul admits uncertainty regarding the nature of this experience. He doesn't know if he was in the physical body or had an out-of-body experience, leaving the question to God's knowledge.

- "such an one caught up to the third heaven." - He describes this individual as having been caught up to the third heaven, signifying a transcendent, heavenly realm beyond the earthly and atmospheric heavens. This suggests a profound spiritual experience.

This verse introduces a mysterious experience of being caught up to a heavenly realm that Paul is about to elaborate on further.

Verse 3 (2 Corinthians 12:3, KJV):

"And I knew such a man, (whether in the body, or out of the body, I cannot tell: God knoweth;)"

Expository Commentary on Verse 3:

In this verse, Paul continues to describe the nature of this mysterious experience.

- "And I knew such a man," - Paul reiterates that he knew the individual who had this extraordinary experience, emphasizing his familiarity with this person.

- "(whether in the body, or out of the body, I cannot tell: God knoweth;)" - Paul restates his uncertainty about the state of the person during this experience, emphasizing that only God knows whether it was in the body or out of the body.

This verse reinforces Paul's emphasis on the mysterious and transcendent nature of the experience he is about to discuss.

Verse 4 (2 Corinthians 12:4, KJV):

"How that he was caught up into paradise, and heard unspeakable words, which it is not lawful for a man to utter."

Expository Commentary on Verse 4:

In this verse, Paul provides further details about the transcendent experience.

- "How that he was caught up into paradise," - Paul reveals that the individual was caught up into paradise, a place associated with the blissful presence of God.

- "and heard unspeakable words," - During this experience, the person heard words and revelations that were so profound and heavenly that they were beyond human expression.

- "which it is not lawful for a man to utter." - Paul emphasizes the sacred and confidential nature of these revelations. They were too holy or too profound to be expressed in human language, and it was not permitted for a person to speak of them.

This verse describes a profound spiritual encounter that included hearing divine words and revelations of exceptional significance.

Verse 5 (2 Corinthians 12:5, KJV):

"Of such an one will I glory: yet of myself I will not glory, but in mine infirmities."

Expository Commentary on Verse 5:

In this verse, Paul decides to boast not about himself but about the person who had this extraordinary experience.

- "Of such an one will I glory:" - Paul expresses his intention to boast about the individual who had the transcendent experience.

- "yet of myself I will not glory," - He distinguishes between boasting about himself and boasting about the other person. He refrains from self-glorification in this context.

- "but in mine infirmities." - Instead, Paul emphasizes that he will boast in his weaknesses and infirmities, a theme he introduced earlier in this letter. This highlights a shift in the focus of his boasting from spiritual experiences to his vulnerabilities and limitations.

This verse underscores Paul's humility and his willingness to highlight the power of Christ in the context of his own weaknesses.

Verse 6 (2 Corinthians 12:6, KJV):

"For though I would desire to glory, I shall not be a fool; for I will say the truth: but now I forbear, lest any man should think of me above that which he seeth me to be, or that he heareth of me."

Expository Commentary on Verse 6:

In this verse, Paul addresses his desire to boast further but shows restraint.

- "For though I would desire to glory," - Paul acknowledges that he has the desire or inclination to boast about his spiritual experiences.

- "I shall not be a fool;" - He recognizes that such boasting might be perceived as foolish, given the extraordinary and supernatural nature of the experiences.

- "for I will say the truth:" - However, he emphasizes that his boasting is truthful and based on actual experiences.

- "but now I forbear," - Despite his desire to continue boasting, he decides to exercise restraint.

- "lest any man should think of me above that which he seeth me to be, or that he heareth of me." - Paul's concern is that people might form an inflated or inaccurate view of him based on his spiritual experiences, exceeding their actual knowledge of him.

This verse reveals Paul's awareness of the potential for misunderstanding and his commitment to truthfulness and humility.

Verse 7 (2 Corinthians 12:7, KJV):

"And lest I should be exalted above measure through the abundance of the revelations, there was given to me a thorn in the flesh, the messenger of Satan to buffet me, lest I should be exalted above measure."

Expository Commentary on Verse 7:

In this verse, Paul shares the reason for the "thorn in the flesh" that he received.

- "And lest I should be exalted above measure through the abundance of the revelations," - Paul explains that to prevent him from becoming excessively prideful due to the abundance of divine revelations and experiences, a specific trial or challenge was given to him.

- "there was given to me a thorn in the flesh," - The metaphorical "thorn in the flesh" represents a significant and persistent challenge or affliction that Paul endured. The nature of this thorn is not explicitly mentioned, and it has been a subject of debate among scholars.

- "the messenger of Satan to buffet me," - The thorn in the flesh is described as a messenger of Satan, suggesting that it may have been a source of affliction or temptation. It was allowed to buffet or harass him.

- "lest I should be exalted above measure." - The purpose of this thorn was to prevent Paul from becoming excessively proud or exalted due to the remarkable revelations he had received.

This verse reveals the divine wisdom behind Paul's affliction and the purpose it served in humbling him and preventing spiritual pride.

Verse 8 (2 Corinthians 12:8, KJV):

"For this thing I besought the Lord thrice, that it might depart from me."

Expository Commentary on Verse 8:

In this verse, Paul describes his earnest prayers to the Lord regarding the removal of the thorn in the flesh.

- "For this thing I besought the Lord thrice," - Paul prayed fervently to the Lord on three separate occasions, pleading for the removal of the affliction or thorn in the flesh.

- "that it might depart from me." - His prayers were specifically focused on the removal of this source of affliction, indicating the distress it caused him.

This verse emphasizes Paul's earnest and repeated petitions to God for relief from his affliction.

Verse 9 (2 Corinthians 12:9, KJV):

"And he said unto me, My grace is sufficient for thee: for my strength is made perfect in weakness. Most gladly, therefore, will I rather glory in my infirmities, that the power of Christ may rest upon me."

Expository Commentary on Verse 9:

In this verse, Paul recounts the response he received from the Lord regarding his request to remove the thorn in the flesh.

- "And he said unto me," - The Lord responded to Paul's entreaty.

- "My grace is sufficient for thee:" - The Lord assured Paul that His grace, or unmerited favor and strength, was enough to sustain him in the midst of his weakness and affliction.

- "for my strength is made perfect in weakness." - The Lord explained that His divine strength is most evident and effective in the midst of human weakness. Weakness provides the context for the manifestation of God's power.

- "Most gladly, therefore, will I rather glory in my infirmities," - In response to this divine assurance, Paul expresses his willingness to boast, not in his spiritual experiences, but in his infirmities and weaknesses.

- "that the power of Christ may rest upon me." - Paul recognizes that it is in his weakness that the power of Christ is most manifest. By boasting in his infirmities, he positions himself for the resting or dwelling of Christ's power upon him.

This verse underscores a profound spiritual principle: God's strength is most evident in human weakness, and Paul willingly embraces his infirmities to experience the power of Christ.

Verse 10 (2 Corinthians 12:10, KJV):

"Therefore, I take pleasure in infirmities, in reproaches, in necessities, in persecutions, in distresses for Christ's sake: for when I am weak, then am I strong."

Expository Commentary on Verse 10:

In this verse, Paul concludes his discussion on the significance of weakness and God's strength.

- "Therefore, I take pleasure in infirmities," - As a result of the divine revelation and assurance he received, Paul now finds joy or pleasure in his infirmities and weaknesses.

- "in reproaches, in necessities, in persecutions, in distresses for Christ's sake:" - He enumerates various forms of suffering and trials that he endures for the sake of Christ, including reproaches (insults), necessities (times of need), persecutions, and distresses.

- "for when I am weak, then am I strong." - Paul summarizes the spiritual truth he has learned: it is in his weakness that the strength of Christ is most evident. Paradoxically, his strength is found in acknowledging and embracing his weaknesses.

This verse encapsulates the core lesson of this passage, emphasizing the transformation of weakness into spiritual strength through reliance on Christ.

In this section of 2 Corinthians 12, Paul shares a profound spiritual experience involving visions and revelations, as well as a significant affliction described as a "thorn in the flesh." He recounts his prayers for the removal of this affliction and the Lord's response, which emphasized the sufficiency of God's grace in weakness. Paul's conclusion is that he takes pleasure in his weaknesses and suffering for the sake of Christ because it is in these moments that he experiences the strength of Christ. This passage illustrates the transformative power of divine grace and the paradoxical nature of strength in weakness.

Verse 11 (2 Corinthians 12:11, KJV):

"I am become a fool in glorying; ye have compelled me: for I ought to have been commended of you: for in nothing am I behind the very chiefest apostles, though I be nothing."

Expository Commentary on Verse 11:

In this verse, Paul addresses the Corinthians' role in his "foolish boasting."

- "I am become a fool in glorying; ye have compelled me:" - Paul acknowledges that he feels like a fool for boasting, and he attributes this behavior to the Corinthians. They have compelled him to engage in this boasting by questioning his authority and apostleship.

- "for I ought to have been commended of you:" - Paul believes that the Corinthians should have commended or endorsed his apostolic authority and ministry. He expected their support and recognition.

- "for in nothing am I behind the very chiefest apostles," - Paul asserts that he is not inferior to the most prominent apostles in any way. He is on par with them in terms of his apostolic authority and ministry.

- "though I be nothing." - Despite his equality with other apostles, Paul humbly acknowledges his own insignificance or unworthiness. He recognizes that any worth or significance he possesses is due to God's grace and the power of Christ.

This verse reveals Paul's complex feelings about boasting. He believes the Corinthians should have commended him, yet he humbly acknowledges his dependence on God's grace.

Verse 12 (2 Corinthians 12:12, KJV):

"Truly the signs of an apostle were wrought among you in all patience, in signs, and wonders, and mighty deeds."

Expository Commentary on Verse 12:

In this verse, Paul offers evidence of his apostolic authority through the signs and wonders that occurred during his ministry among the Corinthians.

- "Truly the signs of an apostle were wrought among you" - Paul declares that the unmistakable signs or marks of an apostle were evident in the Corinthians' midst. These signs validate his apostleship.

- "in all patience," - He emphasizes that these signs occurred with great patience on his part. He was willing to endure difficulties and hardships in his ministry.

- "in signs, and wonders, and mighty deeds." - Paul enumerates the specific signs that accompanied his ministry, including miraculous signs, wonders, and powerful deeds. These extraordinary occurrences testified to the authenticity of his apostleship.

This verse serves as a defense of Paul's apostolic authority by pointing to the supernatural manifestations of God's power in his ministry.

Verse 13 (2 Corinthians 12:13, KJV):

"For what is it wherein ye were inferior to other churches, except it be that I myself was not burdensome to you? forgive me for this wrong."

Expository Commentary on Verse 13:

In this verse, Paul highlights a specific way in which the Corinthians were different from other churches.

- "For what is it wherein ye were inferior to other churches," - Paul questions the Corinthians about how they were inferior or different from other churches. He implies that they were not fundamentally inferior.

- "except it be that I myself was not burdensome to you?" - The distinguishing factor seems to be that Paul did not burden or financially depend on the Corinthians. He did not ask for financial support from them.

- "forgive me this wrong." - Paul appears to ask for forgiveness from the Corinthians for not accepting financial support from them. He addresses this as if it were a wrong or oversight.

This verse underscores the unique financial arrangement between Paul and the Corinthians, as he refrained from being a financial burden to them, which sets them apart from other churches.

In these verses, Paul continues to address the issue of boasting, asserting his apostolic authority through the signs and wonders that accompanied his ministry. He also highlights the unique financial arrangement between him and the Corinthians, expressing a willingness to be forgiven for not being a financial burden to them. Paul's tone in this passage is one of humility and earnestness in defending his apostleship and relationship with the Corinthians.

Verse 14 (2 Corinthians 12:14, KJV):

"Behold, the third time I am ready to come to you; and I will not be burdensome to you: for I seek not yours but you: for the children ought not to lay up for the parents, but the parents for the children."

Expository Commentary on Verse 14:

In this verse, Paul expresses his intentions regarding his upcoming visit to the Corinthians and his attitude towards financial matters.

- "Behold, the third time I am ready to come to you;" - Paul is preparing for his third visit to the Corinthians. He has visited them on two previous occasions, and this visit will be his third.

- "and I will not be burdensome to you:" - Just as he mentioned in the previous verses, Paul reiterates his commitment not to be a financial burden to the Corinthians during his visit.

- "for I seek not yours but you:" - He emphasizes that his primary concern is not their material possessions but their well-being and spiritual growth. He seeks to build a relationship with them, not to profit from them.

- "for the children ought not to lay up for the parents, but the parents for the children." - Paul employs an analogy to describe the appropriate relationship between him as a spiritual father and the Corinthians as his spiritual children. In this analogy, parents provide for their children, not the other way around. He implies that he should be the one giving to them, not the reverse.

This verse reveals Paul's heart for the Corinthians, emphasizing his desire to nurture their spiritual growth and well-being rather than to receive material support from them.

Verse 15 (2 Corinthians 12:15, KJV):

"And I will very gladly spend and be spent for you; though the more abundantly I love you, the less I be loved."

Expository Commentary on Verse 15:

In this verse, Paul further elaborates on his attitude and commitment toward the Corinthians.

- "And I will very gladly spend and be spent for you;" - Paul expresses his willingness to expend himself, both in terms of effort and resources, for the benefit of the Corinthians. He is enthusiastic about sacrificially serving them.

- "though the more abundantly I love you, the less I be loved." - Paul acknowledges a painful reality: the more love and service he pours into the Corinthians, the less love he perceives from them in return. Despite his genuine affection and dedication to their spiritual well-being, he experiences a lack of reciprocal love.

This verse highlights the sacrificial love and commitment of Paul, who is willing to give abundantly to the Corinthians, even when it seems unreciprocated.

Verse 16 (2 Corinthians 12:16, KJV):

"But be it so, I did not burden you: nevertheless, being crafty, I caught you with guile."

Expository Commentary on Verse 16:

In this verse, Paul responds to a potential accusation of deception.

- "But be it so, I did not burden you:" - Paul reiterates that he did not become a financial burden to the Corinthians, confirming his commitment to not seeking financial support from them.

- "nevertheless, being crafty, I caught you with guile." - In a somewhat ironic or sarcastic tone, Paul suggests that some may perceive his actions as crafty or deceitful, as if he used cunning methods to avoid accepting support from the Corinthians.

This verse reveals that Paul is aware of the potential misinterpretations of his actions, but he remains steadfast in his commitment to not burden the Corinthians.

Verse 17 (2 Corinthians 12:17, KJV):

"Did I make a gain of you by any of them whom I sent unto you?"

Expository Commentary on Verse 17:

In this verse, Paul addresses the accusation that he profited from the messengers he sent to the Corinthians.

- "Did I make a gain of you by any of them whom I sent unto you?" - Paul challenges the Corinthians to consider whether he personally benefited or made a profit from any of the individuals he sent to them. He is probing the validity of any allegations that he sought personal gain through his associates.

This verse is a direct question aimed at dispelling any suspicions of financial exploitation on Paul's part.

Verse 18 (2 Corinthians 12:18, KJV):

"I desired Titus, and with him I sent a brother. Did Titus make a gain of you? Walked we not in the same spirit? walked we not in the same steps?"

Expository Commentary on Verse 18:

In this verse, Paul provides an example to challenge any accusations of financial gain.

- "I desired Titus, and with him I sent a brother." - Paul mentions that he sent Titus, a trusted associate, along with another Christian brother, to the Corinthians. These individuals were sent for specific purposes in the Corinthian context.

- "Did Titus make a gain of you?" - He poses a rhetorical question regarding Titus. Did Titus personally profit or gain from the Corinthians during his mission to them?

- "Walked we not in the same spirit? walked we not in the same steps?" - Paul asserts that he and his associates, including Titus, were guided by the same spirit and followed the same principles. Their actions and motives were aligned.

This verse further underlines Paul's integrity and the consistency of his actions and those of his associates, refuting any accusations of personal gain.

In this portion of 2 Corinthians 12, Paul reaffirms his commitment not to burden the Corinthians and expresses his willingness to spend and be spent for their benefit, even if he perceives a lack of reciprocal love. He responds to potential accusations of deception and personal gain, using rhetorical questions and examples to emphasize the integrity of his ministry and the consistency of his actions and those of his associates. This passage reflects Paul's deep concern for the Corinthians and his determination to serve them selflessly.

Verse 19 (2 Corinthians 12:19, KJV):

"Again, think ye that we excuse ourselves unto you? we speak before God in Christ: but we do all things, dearly beloved, for your edifying."

Expository Commentary on Verse 19:

In this verse, Paul addresses the Corinthians' perception of his motives and actions.

- "Again, think ye that we excuse ourselves unto you?" - Paul questions whether the Corinthians believe that he is making excuses or defending himself before them. He seems to be addressing their skepticism regarding his intentions.

- "we speak before God in Christ:" - Paul affirms the sincerity and seriousness of his speech. He speaks before God, invoking the name of

Christ to emphasize the sacredness of his words. He wants to make it clear that he is not merely offering excuses but speaking with a deep sense of responsibility.

- "but we do all things, dearly beloved, for your edifying." - He reassures the Corinthians that everything he does is for their benefit and spiritual growth. His actions are motivated by love and concern for their edification, emphasizing his genuine care for them.

This verse underscores the sincerity of Paul's intentions and actions, expressing his commitment to their spiritual well-being.

Verse 20 (2 Corinthians 12:20, KJV):

"For I fear, lest, when I come, I shall not find you such as I would, and that I shall be found unto you such as ye would not: lest there be debates, envying, wraths, Strifes, backbiting, whisperings, swellings, tumults:"

Expository Commentary on Verse 20:

In this verse, Paul expresses his concerns about the state of the Corinthians when he visits them.

- "For I fear, lest, when I come, I shall not find you such as I would," - Paul is apprehensive that when he arrives in Corinth, he will not find the Corinthians in the spiritual condition he desires. He wishes to see them growing and maturing in their faith.

- "and that I shall be found unto you such as ye would not:" - He is also concerned that when he comes, he might have to take corrective actions that the Corinthians would prefer not to see. He hopes to avoid situations where he needs to exercise discipline or rebuke.

- "lest there be debates, envying, wraths, Strifes, backbiting, whisperings, swellings, tumults:" - Paul lists various negative behaviors and attitudes that he hopes to avoid among the Corinthians. These include contentious debates, jealousy, anger, conflicts, malicious gossip, secret complaints, arrogance, and disturbances.

This verse reflects Paul's pastoral concern for the Corinthians' spiritual well-being and the need to address issues that may hinder their growth.

Verse 21 (2 Corinthians 12:21, KJV):

"And lest, when I come again, my God will humble me among you, and that I shall bewail many which have sinned already and have not repented of the uncleanness and fornication and lasciviousness which they have committed."

Expository Commentary on Verse 21:

In this verse, Paul continues to express his concerns about the Corinthians and their behavior.

- "And lest, when I come again, my God will humble me among you," - Paul fears that when he returns to Corinth, he may be humbled or deeply saddened by what he encounters among the Corinthians. He anticipates that their behavior might grieve him.

- "and that I shall bewail many which have sinned already," - He expects to mourn or grieve over many Corinthians who have already sinned. He is deeply concerned about their spiritual condition.

- "and have not repented of the uncleanness and fornication and lasciviousness which they have committed." - Paul specifies the sins that trouble him, which include impurity, sexual immorality, and lasciviousness (lack of self-control or indulgence in sensual pleasures). He is distressed by the lack of repentance for these sins.

This verse highlights Paul's pastoral responsibility and his desire for the Corinthians to turn away from sinful behavior and to repent.

In this section of 2 Corinthians 12, Paul addresses the Corinthians' perceptions of his motives and expresses his concerns about their behavior and spiritual condition. He emphasizes his commitment to their edification and warns against the presence of negative behaviors and sins that need to be addressed. This passage reveals Paul's pastoral love and concern for the Corinthians' spiritual well-being and the need for spiritual growth and repentance.

Chapter 13
Testing and Self-Examination

The theme of 2 Corinthians Chapter 13 centers on the idea of examination, testing, and self-examination. In this chapter, the apostle Paul encourages the Corinthian believers to examine themselves and test their faith to ensure they are in alignment with the teachings of Christ. He also reiterates his authority as an apostle and warns those who have been causing division and questioning his legitimacy.

Key themes in 2 Corinthians Chapter 13 include:

1. Self-Examination: Paul urges the Corinthians to examine themselves to see whether they are truly in faith. He wants them to assess their own beliefs, attitudes, and actions to ensure they are living in accordance with the teachings of Christ.

2. Spiritual Maturity: The chapter emphasizes the idea of spiritual growth and maturity. Believers are called to grow in their faith, demonstrating the transformative power of the gospel in their lives.

3. Apostolic Authority: Paul asserts his apostolic authority, defending his role as a genuine apostle of Christ. He challenges those who have questioned his legitimacy and warns them about the consequences of their actions.

4. Unity and Reconciliation: While addressing divisions and conflicts within the Corinthian church, the chapter encourages unity and

reconciliation among believers. Paul seeks to restore broken relationships and promote harmony within the Christian community.

5. The Power of Christ: Throughout the chapter, the power of Christ is a recurring theme. Paul emphasizes that it is through Christ's strength that believers can achieve spiritual growth, reconciliation, and unity.

In summary, 2 Corinthians Chapter 13 underscores the importance of self-examination, spiritual growth, and unity within the Corinthian church. It serves as a call to authentic faith, a reminder of the authority of genuine apostles, and a plea for reconciliation and harmony among believers.

Verse 1 (2 Corinthians 13:1, KJV):

"This is the third time I am coming to you. In the mouth of two or three witnesses shall every word be established."

Expository Commentary on Verse 1:

In this verse, Paul mentions his third visit to the Corinthians and references a principle of establishing truth through multiple witnesses.

- "This is the third time I am coming to you." - Paul informs the Corinthians that he is about to make his third visit to them. This underscores the importance of his relationship with the Corinthians and the issues he wants to address.

- "In the mouth of two or three witnesses shall every word be established." - Paul alludes to a biblical principle derived from the Old Testament (Deuteronomy 19:15) regarding the establishment of truth or testimony. In legal matters and disputes, the testimony of two or three witnesses was required to validate a matter. Paul may be hinting at the importance of multiple witnesses in the context of resolving issues and disputes within the Corinthian church.

This verse sets the stage for Paul's impending visit and suggests that he may be bringing witnesses to confirm his words and actions.

Verse 2 (2 Corinthians 13:2, KJV):

"I told you before, and foretell you, as if I were present, the second time; and being absent now I write to them which heretofore have sinned, and to all other, that, if I come again, I will not spare:"

Expository Commentary on Verse 2:

In this verse, Paul recalls his previous warnings to the Corinthians and reaffirms his intention not to spare corrective measures.

- "I told you before, and foretell you, as if I were present, the second time;" - Paul reminds the Corinthians of his previous warnings and exhortations. He speaks with a sense of anticipation and authority, as if he were with them in person, addressing them for the second time.

- "and being absent now I write to them which heretofore have sinned, and to all other," - In his absence, Paul writes to address those who have sinned in the past and to all other members of the Corinthian congregation. He broadens the scope of his message to include the entire church.

- "that, if I come again, I will not spare:" - Paul leaves no room for ambiguity. He makes it clear that if he returns to Corinth and encounters the same issues or sins, he will not spare corrective actions. He is resolute in addressing the problems within the church.

This verse underscores Paul's commitment to addressing the issues of sin and misbehavior within the Corinthian congregation, both in his absence through his letter and in person during his visit.

Verse 3 (2 Corinthians 13:3, KJV):

"Since ye seek a proof of Christ speaking in me, which to you-ward is not weak, but is mighty in you."

Expository Commentary on Verse 3:

In this verse, Paul acknowledges the Corinthians' desire for proof of Christ's presence and authority in his ministry.

- "Since ye seek a proof of Christ speaking in me," - The Corinthians seem to be seeking evidence or proof that Christ is indeed working and speaking through Paul. They want assurance of the authenticity of his apostolic ministry.

- "which to you-ward is not weak but is mighty in you." - Paul affirms that the presence of Christ's power and authority in his ministry is not lacking or weak when it comes to the Corinthians. It has been effective and strong among them.

This verse addresses the Corinthians' desire for proof of Paul's apostolic authority and reinforces the idea that Christ's power is manifested in his ministry among them.

Verse 4 (2 Corinthians 13:4, KJV):

"For though he was crucified through weakness, yet he liveth by the power of God. For we also are weak in him, but we shall live with him by the power of God toward you."

Expository Commentary on Verse 4:

In this verse, Paul draws a parallel between Christ's crucifixion and resurrection and his own ministry.

- "For though he was crucified through weakness," - Paul begins by acknowledging that Christ's crucifixion appeared to be an act of weakness. However, this weakness led to the ultimate victory of the resurrection.

- "yet he liveth by the power of God." - Christ's crucifixion was followed by His resurrection, which demonstrated the power of God. It is through God's power that Christ lives.

- "For we also are weak in him," - Paul relates his own experience of weakness, particularly in the face of the Corinthians' doubts and challenges to his authority.

- "but we shall live with him by the power of God toward you." - Just as Christ was raised by the power of God, Paul expresses confidence that he and his fellow ministers will live with Christ, supported by the power of God, in their ministry among the Corinthians.

This verse underscores the connection between Christ's crucifixion and resurrection, as well as the role of God's power in sustaining Paul and his associates in their ministry.

In this section of 2 Corinthians 13, Paul prepares the Corinthians for his third visit, reaffirms his commitment to addressing issues, and emphasizes the need for evidence of Christ's presence and power in his ministry. He also draws parallels between Christ's crucifixion and resurrection and his own experiences of weakness and divine empowerment. These verses reflect Paul's pastoral concern and his readiness to take corrective actions within the Corinthian church.

Verse 5 (2 Corinthians 13:5, KJV):

"Examine yourselves, whether ye be in the faith; prove your own selves. Know ye not your own selves, how that Jesus Christ is in you, except ye be reprobates?"

Expository Commentary on Verse 5:

In this verse, Paul urges the Corinthians to engage in self-examination regarding their faith and the presence of Christ within them.

- "Examine yourselves, whether ye be in the faith;" - Paul encourages the Corinthians to evaluate and assess their own faith. This self-examination involves scrutinizing the genuineness and vitality of their faith in Christ.

- "prove your own selves." - He calls them to test and prove their own spiritual condition. This involves assessing the authenticity and strength of their relationship with Christ.

- "Know ye not your own selves, how that Jesus Christ is in you," - Paul reminds them that they should be aware of their own spiritual state. He implies that if they are genuine believers, they should recognize the presence of Christ within them through the Holy Spirit.

- "except ye be reprobates?" - Paul suggests that a lack of genuine faith and the absence of Christ's presence within them would indicate a state of reprobation or spiritual rejection.

This verse underscores the importance of self-examination and the evidence of Christ's presence within believers as a test of their faith.

Verse 6 (2 Corinthians 13:6, KJV):

"But I trust that ye shall know that we are not reprobates."

Expository Commentary on Verse 6:

In this verse, Paul expresses his trust that the Corinthians will recognize the authenticity of his ministry.

- "But I trust that ye shall know that we are not reprobates." - Paul places his trust in the Corinthians' ability to discern that he and his fellow ministers are not reprobates or spiritually rejected. He anticipates that they will recognize the legitimacy of his apostolic ministry.

This verse reveals Paul's confidence in the Corinthians' ability to discern the authenticity of his ministry and his desire for them to acknowledge this truth.

Verse 7 (2 Corinthians 13:7, KJV):

"Now I pray to God that ye do no evil; not that we should appear approved, but that ye should do that which is honest, though we be as reprobates."

Expository Commentary on Verse 7:

In this verse, Paul expresses his desire for the Corinthians to do what is right, regardless of how they perceive him and his fellow ministers.

-"Now I pray to God that ye do no evil;" - Paul prays that the Corinthians would refrain from doing any evil or sinful actions. His primary concern is their moral and ethical behavior.

- "not that we should appear approved," - He clarifies that his desire for their righteous conduct is not to make him and his associates appear approved or vindicated. Their goal is the Corinthians' well-being, not their own reputation.

- "but that ye should do that which is honest, though we be as reprobates." - Paul emphasizes that he wants the Corinthians to do what is honest, right, and morally upright, even if they regard him and his colleagues as reprobates. Their actions should be guided by ethical principles, not by perceptions of Paul's ministry.

This verse highlights Paul's emphasis on the Corinthians' ethical conduct and his willingness to prioritize their moral well-being over his own reputation.

Verse 8 (2 Corinthians 13:8, KJV):

"For we can do nothing against the truth, but for the truth."

Expository Commentary on Verse 8:

In this verse, Paul affirms the alignment of his ministry with the truth.

- "For we can do nothing against the truth," - Paul asserts that he and his fellow ministers cannot act against the truth. Their ministry is in harmony with God's truth and the message of the gospel.

- "but for the truth." - He emphasizes that their actions and ministry are directed toward promoting and advancing the truth of God. Everything they do is in support of the truth, not against it.

This verse underscores the integrity of Paul's ministry and his commitment to upholding and promoting the truth of the gospel.

Verse 9 (2 Corinthians 13:9, KJV):

"For we are glad when we are weak and ye are strong: and this also we wish, even your perfection."

Expository Commentary on Verse 9:

In this verse, Paul expresses his joy in the Corinthians' spiritual strength and his desire for their spiritual maturity.

- "For we are glad when we are weak and ye are strong:" - Paul finds joy when he and his fellow ministers appear weak, while the Corinthians are strong in their faith and spiritual growth. He values their spiritual strength.

- "and this also we wish, even your perfection." - He expresses his desire for their spiritual perfection or completeness. Paul longs for their continued growth and maturity in their walk with Christ.

This verse reveals Paul's deep concern for the Corinthians' spiritual well-being and his willingness to prioritize their growth over his own appearance of strength.

Verse 10 (2 Corinthians 13:10, KJV):

"Therefore, I write these things being absent, lest being present I should use sharpness, according to the power which the Lord hath given me to edification, and not to destruction."

Expository Commentary on Verse 10:

In this verse, Paul explains his purpose in writing with a tone of correction.

- "Therefore, I write these things being absent," - Paul clarifies that he is writing these things in his letter while he is physically absent from the Corinthians. He uses his written communication to address issues.

- "lest being present I should use sharpness," - He writes to avoid the necessity of using a sharp or severe tone when he is physically present with the Corinthians. His goal is to minimize the need for strong corrective actions.

- "according to the power which the Lord hath given me to edification, and not to destruction." - Paul reminds the Corinthians that any corrective actions he might take are in line with the authority and power the Lord has given him for the purpose of edification or building the church, not for its destruction.

This verse underscores Paul's pastoral concern and his intention to use his God-given authority for the spiritual growth and edification of the Corinthians, rather than for destructive purposes.

In this section of 2 Corinthians 13, Paul urges the Corinthians to engage in self-examination, emphasizing the need for genuine faith and the presence of Christ within them. He expresses confidence in the Corinthians' ability to discern the authenticity of

his ministry and their moral conduct. Paul also clarifies his desire for their ethical behavior and highlights his ministry's alignment with the truth of the gospel. He expresses joy in their spiritual strength and their continued growth, and he reiterates his commitment to using his authority for their edification rather than their destruction. These verses showcase Paul's pastoral care for the Corinthians and his emphasis on their spiritual well-being.

Verse 11 (2 Corinthians 13:11, KJV):
"Finally, brethren, farewell. Be perfect, be of good comfort, be of one mind, live in peace; and the God of love and peace shall be with you."
Expository Commentary on Verse 11:

In this verse, Paul offers his final words to the Corinthians, providing them with a set of instructions for their Christian walk.
- "Finally, brethren, farewell." - Paul begins by addressing the Corinthians with the term "brethren" and bids them farewell. This is a closing greeting that reflects the conclusion of his letter.

- "Be perfect," - Paul encourages the Corinthians to pursue perfection or maturity in their faith. This perfection does not imply sinless perfection but rather completeness and growth in their Christian walk.

- "be of good comfort," - He advises them to find comfort and encouragement in their faith, relying on the comfort that comes from God's presence.

- "be of one mind," - Paul emphasizes the importance of unity and harmony among the Corinthians. They should be of one mind, sharing the same purpose and goals in their Christian walk.

- "live in peace;" - He urges them to live in peace, promoting a spirit of peace and reconciliation within the Christian community.

- "and the God of love and peace shall be with you." - Paul assures the Corinthians that if they follow these instructions, the God of love and peace will be present with them. Their pursuit of unity and peace aligns with God's nature and character.

This verse provides a positive and encouraging conclusion to Paul's letter, highlighting the themes of maturity, unity, peace, and God's presence.

Verse 12 (2 Corinthians 13:12, KJV):

"Greet one another with a holy kiss."

Expository Commentary on Verse 12:

In this brief verse, Paul instructs the Corinthians to greet one another with a holy kiss.

- "Greet one another with a holy kiss." - Paul encourages the practice of exchanging a holy kiss as a sign of Christian affection and unity. In the cultural context of the time, such a kiss was a common way to express love, friendship, and reconciliation among believers. The term "holy" underscores the sacred and pure nature of this gesture.

This verse emphasizes the importance of warm and affectionate relationships among believers in the Christian community.

In these concluding verses of 2 Corinthians 13, Paul offers his parting words to the Corinthians, urging them to pursue maturity, unity, and peace in their Christian walk. He assures them of God's presence when they follow these instructions. Additionally, he encourages the practice of a holy kiss as a symbol of Christian affection and unity within the faith community. These verses reflect Paul's pastoral concern for the Corinthians' well-being and their relationships within the church.

Verse 13 (2 Corinthians 13:13, KJV):

"All the saints salute you."

Expository Commentary on Verse 13:

In this brief verse, Paul conveys a greeting from all the saints to the Corinthians.

- "All the saints salute you." - Paul informs the Corinthians that all the saints, likely referring to fellow believers and Christians in other places, send their greetings to them. This is a sign of Christian fellowship and solidarity.

This verse is a simple and heartfelt way of connecting the Corinthians with the wider Christian community and emphasizing the sense of unity and shared faith among believers.

In this closing verse of 2 Corinthians 13, Paul conveys the warm greetings of all the saints to the Corinthians, reinforcing the idea of the broader Christian family and the sense of community among believers. It serves as a reminder of the support and fellowship that exist among Christians.

Verse 14 (2 Corinthians 13:14, KJV):

"The grace of the Lord Jesus Christ, and the love of God, and the communion of the Holy Ghost, be with you all. Amen."

Expository Commentary on Verse 14:

In this verse, often referred to as the "Trinitarian Benediction," Paul concludes his second letter to the Corinthians with a profound blessing invoking the Triune God.

- "The grace of the Lord Jesus Christ," - Paul begins by invoking the grace of the Lord Jesus Christ. This signifies the unmerited favor, mercy, and blessing that believers receive through their faith in Jesus. It reflects the central role of Christ's work in our salvation.

- "and the love of God," - The love of God the Father is emphasized here. It represents the deep and unfailing love that God has for His people.

This love is the source of our salvation and the foundation of our relationship with Him.

- "and the communion of the Holy Ghost," - The Holy Spirit is associated with communion, fellowship, and the sharing of divine life with believers. It signifies the Spirit's role in uniting believers with God and with one another.

- "be with you all. Amen." - Paul concludes the benediction with the desire that these divine attributes—grace, love, and communion—be present and active in the lives of all the Corinthians. The "Amen" signifies affirmation and agreement with this heartfelt blessing.

Trinitarian Benediction:

This verse is often referred to as the Trinitarian Benediction because it acknowledges the distinct roles and attributes of each person of the Trinity—God the Father, God the Son, and God the Holy Spirit. It beautifully encapsulates the Christian understanding of the triune nature of God.

- The reference to Jesus Christ reflects the role of the Son in our salvation and the grace extended to us through His sacrifice.

- The reference to God the Father emphasizes His eternal love, the source of all blessings.

- The reference to the Holy Spirit underscores His role in uniting believers with the divine and with one another.

This benediction serves as a fitting conclusion to Paul's letter, invoking the fullness of God's blessings upon the Corinthians and all believers. It reminds us of the inseparable and harmonious work of the Triune God in the lives of His people.

In this closing verse of 2 Corinthians 13, Paul invokes a powerful Trinitarian blessing, highlighting the grace of Jesus Christ, the love of God the Father, and the communion of the Holy Spirit. It serves as a reminder of the foundational Christian doctrine of the Trinity and the rich blessings that believers receive through their faith in God.

CONCLUSION

The conclusion of 2 Corinthians marks the culmination of the apostle Paul's heartfelt and pastoral communication with the Corinthian church. Throughout this letter, Paul has addressed various issues, including the nature of his ministry, the collection for saints, his subjective experiences, and the challenges he has faced. In this concluding section, he leaves the Corinthians with important exhortations and reminders that encapsulate the essence of his message.

Paul expresses his hope that the Corinthians will heed his advice and continue to grow in their faith and maturity. He desires that they strive for unity and reconciliation within the church, aiming to restore any broken relationships. The apostle underscores the importance of living in harmony with one another, reminding the Corinthians that God is the God of love and peace, and His presence should be reflected in their community.

He reaffirms his appreciation for the Corinthians' faithfulness and willingness to partner with him in ministry. He commends their generosity and encourages them to complete the collection for the saints in Jerusalem, an act of love and support for their fellow believers in need. Paul also highlights the significance of joyful giving and the blessings that come from a generous and cheerful heart.

Paul's closing words emphasize the Trinitarian nature of God—Father, Son, and Holy Spirit—and the rich blessings that believers receive through their relationship with Him. He offers a Trinitarian benediction, invoking the grace of the Lord Jesus Christ, the love of God the Father, and the communion of the Holy Spirit upon the Corinthians. This benediction underscores the central role of the Triune God in the life of the Christian community and serves as a reminder of the foundational Christian doctrine of the Trinity.

In his final exhortations, Paul urges the Corinthians to be watchful and discerning, aware of Satan's schemes that could disrupt their unity and faith. He emphasizes the importance of forgiveness and reconciliation, illustrating his pastoral care for their spiritual well-being. This is a reminder of the ongoing spiritual battle that believers face and the necessity of vigilance and spiritual maturity in the face of adversity.

Paul concludes his letter with a strong appeal for the Corinthians to examine themselves and their faith, ensuring that they are in alignment with the teachings of Christ. He reminds them that the power of Christ resides in them, and their faith should reflect this power. He envisions a church marked by unity, love, and spiritual strength.

In the closing verses of 2 Corinthians, the apostle Paul leaves the Corinthians with a sense of encouragement, hope, and guidance. His words emphasize the central themes of faith, love, reconciliation, and the transformative power of the gospel. They provide a fitting conclusion to a letter that is both a testament to his pastoral care for the Corinthians and a rich source of Christian teaching and exhortation. Paul's words continue to resonate with believers, inspiring them to embrace the principles of faith, love, and unity in their own Christian journey.

www.ingramcontent.com/pod-product-compliance
Lightning Source LLC
Chambersburg PA
CBHW061250120726

48001CB00001B/239